Religion and Environmentalism

Recent titles in Religion in Politics and Society Today

Islam in America: Exploring the Issues
Craig Considine

Religion and Environmentalism

Exploring the Issues

Lora Stone

Religion in Politics and Society Today

An Imprint of ABC-CLIO, LLC
Santa Barbara, California • Denver, Colorado

Library of Congress Cataloging-in-Publication Data

Names: Stone, Lora, author.
Title: Religion and environmentalism : exploring the issues / Lora Stone.
Description: First edition. | Santa Barbara, California : ABC-CLIO, an imprint of ABC-CLIO, LLC, [2020] | Series: Religion in politics and society today | Includes bibliographical references and index.
Identifiers: LCCN 2019057088 (print) | LCCN 2019057089 (ebook) | ISBN 9781440868566 (hardcover) | ISBN 9781440868573 (ebook)
Subjects: LCSH: Human ecology—Religious aspects. | Environmentalism—Religious aspects. | Environmental responsibility—Religious aspects.
Classification: LCC BL65.E36 S86 2020 (print) | LCC BL65.E36 (ebook) | DDC 201/.77—dc23
LC record available at https://lccn.loc.gov/2019057088
LC ebook record available at https://lccn.loc.gov/2019057089

ISBN: 978-1-4408-6856-6 (print)
       978-1-4408-6857-3 (ebook)

24 23 22 21 20   1 2 3 4 5

This book is also available as an eBook.

ABC-CLIO
An Imprint of ABC-CLIO, LLC

ABC-CLIO, LLC
147 Castilian Drive
Santa Barbara, California 93117
www.abc-clio.com

This book is printed on acid-free paper ∞

Manufactured in the United States of America

Contents

Alphabetical List of Entries

Topical List of Entries

Environmental Issues
Biodiversity
Climate Change
Deforestation
Energy
Food Security
Hydraulic Fracturing
Marine Conservation
Overpopulation
Pollution
Soil Conservation
Sustainability
Water

Individuals
Bartholomew I of Constantinople
Dalai Lama
Francis of Assisi
Pope Francis I
Shiva, Vandana
Teilhard de Chardin, Pierre
White, Lynn Townsend, Jr.

International Initiatives and Documents
Assisi Declarations
Laudato Si'
Paris Agreement

Organizations
Alliance of Religions and
    Conservation
Evangelical Environmental
    Network
Green Pilgrimage Network
Interfaith Power and Light
Islamic Foundation for Ecology
    and Environmental Sciences
National Religious Partnership for
    the Environment
World Council of Churches

Philosophical Approaches
Ecofeminism
Religious Naturalism

Practices
Environmental Justice
Socially Responsible Investment
Vegetarianism

Religious Traditions
Buddhism
Christianity
Daoism
Hinduism
Islam

Series Foreword

Religion is a pervasive and powerful force in modern society, and its influence on political structures and social institutions is inescapable, whether in the United States or around the world. Wars have been fought in the name of faith; national boundaries have been shaped as a result; and social policies, legislation, and daily life have all been shaped by religious beliefs. Written with the reference needs of high school students and undergraduates in mind, the books in this series examine the role of religion in contemporary politics and society. While the focus of the series is on the United States, it also explores social and political issues of global significance.

Each book in the series is devoted to a particular issue, such as antisemitism, atheism and agnosticism, and women in Islam. An overview essay surveys the development of the religious dimensions of the subject and discusses how religion informs contemporary discourse related to that issue. A chronology then highlights the chief events related to the topic. This is followed by a section of alphabetically arranged reference entries providing objective information about people, legislation, ideas, movements, events, places, and other specific subjects. Each entry cites works for further reading and in many cases provides cross-references. At the end of each volume is an annotated bibliography of the most important print and electronic resources suitable for student research.

Authoritative and objective, the books in this series give readers a concise introduction to the dynamic interplay of religion and politics in modern society and provide a starting point for further research on social issues.

Preface

Religion and Environmentalism: Exploring the Issues provides an introduction to religiously motivated environmentalism, the contemporary environmental issues addressed by religious and spiritual traditions, and relevant organizations, individuals, and initiatives. Major world religions, folk religions, Indigenous spiritual traditions, nature religions, and newly formed or revived religions have all become increasingly involved in environmental issues over the last several decades. During this time, individuals and organizations motivated by their religious and spiritual beliefs have become involved in public discourse on environmental issues, have influenced environmental policies, and have launched diverse initiatives that protect and preserve the natural environment.

Since their earliest cultures, humans have defined their connection to the natural environment through spiritual traditions, religions, and belief systems. In the natural environment there were unseen forces, physically apparent phenomena, and numerous creatures and living things that impacted the daily lives of all people. The earliest sacred stories and practices around the world include explanations about the creation, existence, and purpose of all living things, natural landscapes, waterscapes, and skyscapes, and often the expansive cosmos. These stories and practices provide the foundation for most religiously motivated environmentalism, through new interpretations of ancient sacred texts, practices, beliefs and values, or recommitment to ancient spiritual knowledge.

By exploring their roots, religious and spiritual traditions have rediscovered their connections to the natural environment and embraced a religiously motivated environmentalism. Followers of these traditions are now thinking about environmentalism and ecology in new and exciting ways. Religiously motivated environmentalists are increasingly collaborating with scholars, theorists, scientists, and activists, as well as governments and politicians, on projects and campaigns that protect and preserve the natural environment. Conflicts and disagreements still occur between different religious groups, and between secular values and religious values, but overall there has been a remarkable effort to set aside differences and cooperate on environmental issues.

This book invites the reader to explore the many ways that religious and spiritual traditions are increasingly involved in religiously motivated environmentalism, through political and social action, organizations, policies, and collaborative initiatives. The rise of contemporary religiously motivated environmentalism is documented throughout this book, which includes an introduction that explains concepts and terms, fifty-three entries on topics related to religion and environmentalism, and an annotated bibliography. The entries provide a foundation for understanding religion and environmentalism in a global contemporary context, with suggestions for further reading and an annotated bibliography, all of which lead to a wealth of related literature, research, and scholarship.

Acknowledgments

This work was possible because of the individuals, organizations, and traditions involved with religiously motivated environmentalism, as well as the interest and support of ABC-CLIO editors. The world's many religious and spiritual traditions, the followers of these traditions, environmental activists, scientists, academics and researchers, students, and the general reading public all participate in deepening our understanding of the relationship between humans and their habitats.

Additionally, as a scholar, writer, and researcher, I would like to thank the University of New Mexico both for its expansive library system and its accommodations for faculty involved in publication and research. Numerous colleagues have also supported my interest in social movements and religiously motivated environmentalism over the years, most notably Robert Fiala and Felipe Gonzales.

On a more personal level, I must acknowledge my mother, Linda. Her playful approach to learning nurtured my love of knowledge beginning in my earliest years. She is also responsible for my curiosity about the natural world, spirituality, and religious traditions. She provided opportunities for many adventures in these fields that led to a deep appreciation of the many ways that humans interact with the natural environment.

Overview

Defining Religion and Environmentalism

Historically, humans have developed religions, spiritual traditions, and belief systems that defined their relationships with the natural world as well as their place in the cosmos and their reasons for existence. Religious and spiritual traditions have also shaped collective identity, provided group cohesion, established ethical and moral codes, and enacted sacred rituals for significant events. Additionally, religion and spirituality are intertwined with political power, laws, territory, and, more recently, concepts of progress and global citizenship. In the past, emerging religions were geographically localized, with some eventually spreading around the world through migration and colonization, while others remained tied to a specific place, culture, and people.

As our understanding of religion has expanded, so have the definitions used by scholars, researchers, theologians, and adherents of religions. Although there is no agreement on any one definition of religion, there are some themes that have persisted historically, such as the perceived distinction between religion as a social institution and spirituality as the subjective, lived experience of individuals. Early research in the social sciences, such as Emile Durkheim's *The Elementary Forms of Religious Life* (1912), investigated the functions and structure of religions, including the distinction between the sacred and the profane, as well as the social cohesion provided by collective religious identity. Representative of subsequent scholarship, David Chidester (2001) defined religion as the "dimension of human experience engaged with sacred norms, which are related to transformative forces and powers and which people consider to be dangerous and/or beneficent and/or meaningful in some ultimate way".

The definition of religion has continued to change as scholars and researchers learn more about the functions of religion as well as peoples' diverse experiences with religion. In the twenty-first century, scholars have further broadened the definition of religion to reflect this growth in knowledge and understanding. Benson Saler and other social scientists who study religion have suggested taking a "polyfocal" approach that recognizes all types of religious phenomena, including those with "family resemblances" to religion. Drawing from the research of Chidester, Saler, and others, Bron Taylor advocates in *Dark Green Religion* (2010) for including "religion-resembling" phenomena in the study of religion. Taylor's expanded definition includes localized Indigenous belief systems, major world religions, cults, nature religions, reconstructed Paganism, and radical environmentalist spirituality, among others. It is Taylor's definition that guides interpretations of religion as a category in this book, *Religion and Environmentalism: Exploring the Issues*. Taylor's analysis of religion is representative of current scholarly trends in studies of religion and spirituality that attempt a broad, inclusive understanding of the vast, diverse, and complex field of human religious and spiritual traditions.

Many religions have blended with other belief systems and traditions, as different populations and groups experienced colonization, merged, or traded with each other. Although historically religions provided authoritative explanations of the world, such as the origins of life, the structure of society, and the nature of life itself, this authority became increasingly challenged in recent centuries. Scientific explanations supplanted many religious authoritative explanations, and discoveries in emerging scientific fields such as biology, geology, and physics added to verifiable knowledge about the world and all its life-forms. In the twentieth century, science and religion competed for authority on several issues, such as the status of humans in relation to other species, humanity's role in protecting the natural environment, and the expansion of human populations globally.

As human societies industrialized and expanded, they placed increasing demands on the natural environment. Wilderness areas have been leveled for agricultural use, water sources diverted into resource-intensive farming and livestock enterprises, and parcels of land increasingly appropriated as infrastructure expanded for public utilities, transportation, and communication. This expansion, which included colonization around the world, was often supported by religious ideas, such as rulers being divinely chosen, humans as a species divinely awarded domination of the natural environment, and humans having a divine commandment to increase their populations. By the end of the nineteenth century, urban centers around the world and vast networks of economic colonies were consuming natural resources and ecosystems at unsustainable rates. The dramatic expansion of human populations, their built infrastructures, food and water supply systems, and increased economic development and global trade were supported in part, at least initially, by specific religious beliefs and ideas. Although wondrous economic, scientific, and technological developments have resulted from this expansion, the approach to natural resources was unsustainable, and the impact on the natural environment, ecosystems, and colonized peoples was often devasting.

By the mid-nineteenth century, a modern conservation movement was emerging that was based on scientific management and sustainability of natural resources, such as timber forests, fisheries, wildlife, and wilderness areas. During the late nineteenth and early twentieth centuries, both the British and U.S. governments were adopting conservationist policies that placed natural resources under government protection and regulated private industries' use of these resources. Several political leaders in the early twentieth century, such as U.S. presidents Theodore Roosevelt (1901–1909) and Woodrow Wilson (1913–1921), implemented policies to ensure that natural resources would be sufficient to meet future national needs. During this time, political leaders in several countries were also committed to preserving wildlife and wilderness areas by creating national parks, game preserves for hunting, and bird sanctuaries.

By the 1950s there was a growing divergence in the United States between conservationists, who viewed the natural environment in terms of human needs, and protectionists or preservationists, who viewed the natural world as inherently valuable regardless of human needs. Over the next decade, the environmentalist movement that was coalescing in the United States adopted a protectionist view of the natural environment and in some ways was ideologically distinct from the earlier conservation movement. This distinct environmental movement has also been referred to as the ecology movement, especially in Europe and other regions outside the United States. Around the world, there has been much overlap between the interests, goals, and membership of conservation, ecology, and environmental movements. Since its emergence in the late 1960s, the environmentalist movement has included various organizations and individuals with a range of commitment levels, strategies, and goals. Additionally, it has been primarily a secular movement, grounded in science and data-driven evidence, that is critical of ideologies that value human expansion over preservation of the natural environment.

Historically, several religious traditions around the world have included the belief that humans are superior to all other species. Religions have also been involved in colonization, have supported human population growth, and have often taught that the natural environment was created to fulfill human needs. Beginning in the late 1960s, a growing number of activists, scholars, and scientists asserted that religions and religious ideas had been major contributors to the contemporary environmental crisis, resulting in the destruction, degradation, and overdevelopment of the natural world. In response to both this secular criticism and their own concern for the natural world, many theologians, religious organizations, and religiously motivated activists became increasingly involved in environmental issues. Additionally, both existing and reconstructed, nature-based belief systems increasingly emphasized values and lifestyles based in environmentalism. In recent decades, religiously motivated environmentalism has become a powerful force in shaping environmental policy and activism globally, and it has joined with secular environmentalism to address issues.

Secular and Religious Environmentalism

Although it has roots in the secular environmental movement that began in the 1960s, the religious environmental movement did not formally emerge until the 1990s. The earlier secular environmental movement provided a base of knowledge, including strategies for mobilizing public support, organizing direct action, and working with governments and policy agencies. The early secular environmental movement also identified core issues and introduced these issues into local, regional, and global organizations. Initially, many religious adherents and secular environmentalists struggled to find common ground regarding beliefs and motivation. Some secular environmentalists believed that organized religion sought to dominate nature or encouraged behaviors that destroyed the natural environment. On the other hand, some religious traditions and their followers were concerned that secular environmentalists held views that were in opposition to various religious teachings, such as doctrines, beliefs, or practices involving reproduction, gender equality, and personhood.

In actuality, many religious traditions have historically had beliefs and practices that included a spiritual and sustainable relationship with the natural environment, while others have held that the world was created to fulfill human needs. Some religions have sacred texts or practices that emphasize an interdependence among all living things and elements of creation. This emphasis on the interconnection of all life has often been seen as a characteristic of Asian or Eastern religious traditions such as Buddhism, Confucianism, Hinduism, Jainism, Shinto, Sikhism, and Daoism. In contrast, the Abrahamic or monotheistic religions have often been typified as anthropocentric, focused on the relationship between humans and God, and inclined toward human domination of nature. Various academics and activists have asserted that the Asian religious traditions, folk religions, and Indigenous belief systems have core beliefs and practices similar to those of the emerging secular environmental movement. Conversely, the Abrahamic and monotheistic religious traditions have been associated with empire building, colonialism, and industrialism, and are thought to be inclined to dominate or ravage the natural world. In reality, the history of religions and the natural environment is extremely complex, with much variation by region, historical period, and circumstance within all religious traditions and belief systems.

In the late 1960s, the Judeo-Christian tradition specifically was criticized both for a purported role historically in the destruction of the natural world and for its belief in a divinely mandated human domination of nature. An article in *Science* representative of this criticism, Lynn Townsend White Jr. (1967), was widely read throughout the late 1960s and in subsequent decades. White's critical article prompted written responses, reflection, inquiry, and action in the Abrahamic traditions, and it continues to be cited today in many studies that examine religion and environmentalism. The first responses defending the Judeo-Christian tradition came in the late 1960s from North American Jewish scholars and were soon followed by responses from Christian scholars, both of whom would contribute to the nascent religious environmental movement. In addition to Jewish and Christian responses, by the 1980s Muslim philosophers and scholars were increasingly noting that there were shared values between Islam and modern environmentalism. By the 1990s all religions in the Abrahamic tradition were involved in a distinctly religious environmental movement that had its roots in the contemporary secular environmental movement that had emerged in the 1960s.

Although there are numerous Asian religious traditions discussed later in this book, Hinduism and Buddhism can provide initial insight into how the natural environment is viewed in these traditions in general. The interdependence of all life and the sanctity of nature are important core tenets of Hinduism. However, adherents of Hinduism have only recently begun, with some exceptions, to put their beliefs into practice as part of a religious environmental movement that shares goals with the secular environmental movement. Within Buddhism, some communities clearly recognized the threat of industrialism to the natural environment by the beginning of the twentieth century. As with Hinduism, however, Buddhism did not develop organized political engagement of environmental issues until after the 1960s, as globalization spread the strategies, tactics, and networks of the secular environmental movement. Although grounded in ancient texts that clearly support a belief in the interdependence of all life and beings, both Buddhism's and Hinduism's formal involvement in environmentalism emerged after exposure to the distinct influences of the secular environmental movement and globalization.

In addition to the Abrahamic and Asian religious traditions, there are many other religious and spiritual belief systems that also began focusing on environmental issues by the end of the twentieth century. Folk and Indigenous religions, usually associated with a specific region, ethnicity, tribe, or traditional knowledge, often have practices and beliefs that involve a close relationship with the natural environment. Some scholars and activists have associated folk and Indigenous religions with traditional ecological knowledge (TEK) that promotes environmentalist values. In the late twentieth century, these folk and Indigenous religions, the Abrahamic and Asian religious traditions, and numerous newly emerging or reconstructed belief systems all began contributing in some way to the contemporary religious environmental movement. In the last few decades, religious traditions have increasingly applied their core beliefs and values to environmental issues, collaborating across traditions and creating organizations that have become part of the religious environmental movement.

From the late 1960s to the present, many religious traditions have reviewed their sacred texts and practices with the hope of understanding the role of religion in environmental issues such as climate change, sustainability, pollution, and ecological degradation. By the 1980s many religious traditions globally were developing philosophical or theological guidelines for organized engagement with regard to environmental issues. Despite having different approaches to the natural world, many religions around the world had contributed to the emergence of a contemporary religious environmental movement by the 1990s. During this time, from the 1960s to the 1990s, religious environmental organizations were being created, alliances were formed among adherents from different belief systems and faith traditions, and a distinct religious environmental movement emerged.

Because the religious environmental movement draws its membership and support from religious communities, issues in this movement are always presented in the ethical or theological framework of religious traditions. World religions, folk religions, and Indigenous belief traditions have all contributed in some way to the emergence, rise, and establishment of the religious environmental movement. Additionally, in the twenty-first century, both the secular and the religious environmental movements have set aside many ideological differences and collaborated on shared goals, and they frequently work together to address local, national, and global environmental issues.

The Religious Environmental Movement

Social movements, including the environmental movement, are organized group efforts that support, encourage, or resist changes in society. Social movements have established, enduring organizational structures that include defined goals, tasks, positions, strategies, intentional behavior, and planned actions. Social movements often continue over several generations and can occur as a series of waves, as participation rises and falls from one decade to the next. All social movements begin with emergence, when a group of people share the perception that something is wrong. After emergence, the core members define and make public the goals of the movement, which is followed by development of the movement's organizational or bureaucratic structure. Over time, a movement might decline if it achieves its goals, experiences organizational problems, loses leadership, or is the target of government-sponsored repression. Sometimes social movements do not decline but rather go through a series of waves, merge with other movements, or revise their goals to meet new challenges. All social movements are political, including the environmental movement and the more recently emerged religious environmental movement, in that they seek to change social norms as well as create, reform, or replace existing public policy.

The religious environmental movement, like all social movements, is a network of groups and organizations that have forged a collective identity based on common concerns and grievances. In general, social movements are more likely to achieve their goals if activists and organizers are able to link together groups that already have skills, shared beliefs, and established social relationships. Social movements can benefit from religions, since religion groups tend to have the experienced leaders, shared cultural elements, strong social relationships, and collective identities that help movements mobilize and achieve their goals. When a distinct religious environmental movement emerged by the 1990s, it expanded quickly because of the many cultural and social resources found in most religions. By the late twentieth century, many religious and spiritual traditions had established formal interreligious relationships that soon served as a foundation for collaboration on environmental concerns and initiatives. The religious environmental movement that emerged in the late twentieth century continues to influence organizations addressing current environmental issues. Similarly, religious beliefs and values in general provide powerful motivation for many people involved in the politics surrounding contemporary environmental issues.

Politics, as a social institution, provides a model for authority, collective decision-making, formalization of a society's goals, and the exercise of individual and collective power. Political participation includes community service, protesting, writing letters, advocacy, membership in organizations, and providing leadership, as well as voting and campaigning. Religion, as a social institution, shapes the norms, beliefs, values, and practices of adherents and builds social relationships through established patterns of interaction. Because political behavior is based in norms, beliefs, and values, people's political participation and understanding of power are often influenced by religion and similar types of belief systems. Scholars of religious social movements have noted that religious beliefs provide motives for political participation and that religious organizations are composed of enduring social relationships that can facilitate political engagement. Increasingly, religions are addressing the environmental consequences of human activities and are involved in creating policies and initiatives that protect the natural environment. Around the world, religious traditions are involved in both collaborative and contentious politics, and they often bring insight, enduring social networks, and experience to efforts aimed at resolving contemporary environmental issues and concerns.

Over the last few decades, activists, institutional leaders, and other members of diverse religious and spiritual traditions have formed organizations and networks dedicated to religiously motivated environmentalism. Organizations like Interfaith Power and Light (IPL), the Evangelical Environmental Network (EEN), and the Islamic Foundation for Ecology and Environmental Sciences (IFEES) promote political participation and provide education, training, and research on environmental issues. Some religious organizations and networks collaborate with politicians at the national level, such as the National Religious Partnership on the Environment, in the United States, and the Save Ganga Movement, in India. Similarly, leaders of major world religions, such as Pope Francis I and Patriarch Bartholomew I of Constantinople, have formally addressed environmental issues, including climate change and sustainability, at the United Nations, World Bank, and World Health Organization. Other religiously motivated environmental organizations, such as A Rocha Kenya (ARK) and Interfaith Oceans, have increasingly collaborated with scientists, conservationists, and secular activists on initiatives aimed at environmental sustainability. Religiously motivated environmentalism also includes radical activism, such as Indigenous communities protesting hydraulic fracking, and sustainable agriculture activist Vandana Shiva's criticism of unsustainable corporate agriculture.

Entry Categories

Acknowledging the historical backdrop of the religious environmental movement, this volume provides an introductory overview of religion and environmentalism in the twentieth and twenty-first centuries, with an emphasis on representing diverse religious traditions from around the world. It covers several religious traditions, provides a global perspective, and highlights the connections, similarities, and collaborations among the different religious traditions and their involvement in environmentalism. Although different perspectives, beliefs, and theories are discussed, they are presented in a way that emphasizes descriptions and examples rather than advocating a specific position regarding the relationship between religion, politics, and environmentalism. The approach in this book does assume that religion, politics, and environmentalism interact in complex ways, often in collaboration, sometimes contentiously, but almost always with shared concern about core environmental issues. The introduction, entries, annotated bibliography, and index allow for readers to understand the general context of the subject matter, easily locate related readings or topics, and find specific subjects or names of interest. The entries cover religious traditions, important leaders, organizations, institutions, movements, concepts, events, and documents, with each entry including recommendations for further reading at both introductory and more advanced levels.

Buddhism, Christianity, Daoism, Hinduism, Islam, Jainism, Judaism, Shinto, Sikhism, and Paganism all have dedicated entries. Each of these entries provides a general description of the specific religious tradition, a historical overview of its view of nature or the natural environment, a discussion of the tradition's approach to environmental issues, and representative contemporary examples of its involvement in environmentalism. Additionally, there are entries for the general categories of animism, folk religions, nature religions, and traditional ecological knowledge (TEK), all of which are important in contemporary discussions and scholarship about religion and environmentalism. Although not exhaustive, these entries on religious traditions and related general categories offer broad coverage that will provide a foundation for both introductory and more advanced scholars of religion and environmentalism. The case studies and examples in each of these entries also help the reader develop an informed understanding of how the natural environment is viewed around the world by a wide range of religious and spiritual traditions.

There are several entries for core environmental issues, with each of these entries including a definition of the issue, related data and scientific research, and various religious responses to the issue. Biodiversity, climate change, deforestation, energy, food security, hydraulic fracturing, marine conservation, overpopulation, pollution, soil conservation, sustainability, and water all have dedicated entries. Some of these, such as climate change and biodiversity, focus on the official positions and political involvement of major religious institutions and interreligious networks. Other entries, such as soil conservation and hydraulic fracturing, focus on the religiously motivated activism of key individuals and specific communities. In a few entries, such as the entry on overpopulation, recent statistics for major world religions and folk religions are included. In each entry, there is a clear description of the issue based on current scientific knowledge, followed by an overview of how the issue has been perceived by various religious traditions. Additionally, religious communities, scientists, and environmental activists have worked together to address some issues, such as marine conservation, and those types of collaborative efforts are discussed in several entries.

This volume also includes several entries on social movements, theories, branches of theology, and practices that are elements of religiously motivated environmentalism. The religious environmental movement, the New Age movement, religious naturalism, and vegetarianism have entries that provide historical background, discussion of significant trends and individuals, and explanations of their relevancy to religion and environmentalism. Although many entries throughout the book identify important theoretical and philosophical theories, the Gaia hypothesis and the greening of religion hypothesis each have dedicated entries because of their influence. Ecofeminism, ecotheology, and environmental justice can be seen as theoretical approaches, frameworks, or concepts, depending on the context, but all are significant in the history and development of the religious environmental movement. Each one of these topics has an entry that includes a definition, seminal thinkers, and its importance to religion and environmentalism. The term *socially responsible investment* refers both to a concept and a practice, and it also has a dedicated entry because of its frequent use in religious organizations and its impact on environmentally sustainable economic investments.

Several individuals have been selected as representative of important influences or shifts in religiously motivated environmentalism, with the acknowledgement that countless others have had an impact as well. An entry is dedicated to the historian Lynn Townsend White Jr., whom many scholars credit with sparking an important discussion in the 1960s about the relationship between various religions and the natural environment. Pierre Teilhard de Chardin is included because he is considered one of the primary inspirations for ecotheology, a theological approach focused on religion, nature, and environmentalism. The entry for Vandana Shiva, a global leader in sustainable agriculture, is representative of many contemporary individuals engaged in radical environmentalism based in both religion and science. Bartholomew I of Constantinople, Pope Francis I, and Tenzin Gyatso, the 14th Dalai Lama, each have an entry, because of their continuing global influence and their commitment to environmental issues and policies. Francis of Assisi (ca. 1181–1226), whose teachings continue to inspire global, interreligious environmentalist efforts, such as the Assisi Declarations, in 1986, and Pope Francis's encyclical *Laudato Si'*, in 2015, also has a dedicated entry.

For decades there have been events and initiatives that resulted in accompanying documents that are important to religiously motivated environmentalism. Many of these documents are mentioned in various entries throughout this volume. Of the documents, the Assisi Declarations, *Laudato Si'*, and the Paris Agreement have dedicated entries because of their significance, although there are innumerable additional examples since the emergence of the religious environmental movement. The Assisi Declarations is a 1986 document, written by leaders of world religions, that discusses the role of religion in protecting and saving the natural world from environmental crisis. *Laudato Si': On Care for Our Common Home*, a 184-page, 2015 encyclical by Pope Francis I, asserts that environmental degradation and global warming, among other problems, are the consequence of consumerism and irresponsible economic development. The Paris Agreement, approved by the UN in 2016 and created under the auspices of the United Nations Framework Convention on Climate Change (UNFCCC), was endorsed by religious leaders from around the world who showed their support in their 2016 "Interfaith Climate Change Statement to World Leaders."

Over the past few decades, thousands of religious organizations have emerged as part of the religious environmental movement. Several of these organizations have entries in this volume, with each entry providing a description, historical overview, and examples of initiatives and political engagement. The Alliance of Religions and Conservation (ARC), Evangelical Environmental Network (EEN), Green Pilgrimage Network (GPN), Interfaith Power and Light (IPL), Islamic Foundation for Ecology and Environmental Sciences (IFEES), National Religious Partnership for the Environment (NRPE), and the World Council of Churches (WCC) all have separate entries. ARC, GPN, IPL, and NRPE are interreligious organizations with members from diverse religious traditions and a range of goals and initiatives. EEN, IFEES, and WCC are representative of organizations that have been very active in environmentalism over several decades, with each drawing their membership exclusively from a specific religious tradition. The entries in this category introduce readers to religious organizations that are committed to environmentalism in the twenty-first century, have impacted environmental policy, and continue to have regional and global influence.

The entries in this volume cover religious and spiritual traditions, individuals, organizations, movements, theories, practices, and documents, providing readers with an overview of religion and environmentalism. The entries include definitions, historical background, discussions of related scholarship and research, and examples of relevant experiences from around the world. Religious and spiritual traditions are increasingly involved in environmental justice issues, environmental policies, and the management of natural resources. Similarly, there are growing numbers of religious organizations involved in creating environmental policy and advocating for environmental sustainability at all levels of human society. Religious groups that initially did not prioritize environmental issues have, over the past few decades, examined their sacred traditions and ascertained that protecting and preserving the natural environment is a moral imperative. Additionally, numerous religious groups that have historically practiced environmental sustainability have become even more involved in addressing environmental issues. Overall, in many religious and spiritual traditions, the trend in the twenty-first century is toward an expansion of religiously motivated environmentalism and the religious environmental movement.

Further Reading

Chidester, David. 2001. *Patterns of Action: Religion and Ethics in a Comparative Perspective*. Belmont, CA: Wadsworth.

Durkheim, Emile. 1912. *The Elementary Forms of the Religious Life*. London: G. Allen & Unwin.

Ellingson, Stephen. 2016. *To Care for Creation: The Emergence of the Religious Environmental Movement*. Chicago: University of Chicago Press.

Francis, Pope. 2015. *Praise Be to You: Laudato Si': On Care for Our Common Home*. San Francisco: Ignatius Press.

Gade, Anna M. 2019. *Muslim Environmentalisms: Religious and Social Foundations*. New York: Columbia University Press.

Klein, Daniel R., María Pía Carazo, Meinhard Doelle, Jane Bulmer, and Andrew Higham, eds. 2017. *The Paris Agreement on Climate Change: Analysis and Commentary*. Oxford: Oxford University Press.

Sahliyeh, Emile F. 1990. *Religious Resurgence and Politics in the Contemporary World*. SUNY Series in Religion, Culture, and Society. Albany: State University of New York Press.

Saler, Benson. 2000. *Conceptualizing Religion: Immanent Anthropologists, Transcendent Natives, and Unbounded Categories*. New York: Berghahn Books.

Shafiq, Muhammad, and Thomas Herrold Donlin-Smith, eds. 2018. *Nature and the Environment in Contemporary Religious Contexts*. Newcastle upon Tyne, UK: Cambridge Scholars Publishing.

Tarrow, Sidney G. 2011. *Power in Movement: Social Movements and Contentious Politics*. Cambridge Studies in Comparative Politics. New York: Cambridge University Press.

Taylor, Bron Raymond. 2010. *Dark Green Religion: Nature Spirituality and the Planetary Future*. Berkeley: University of California Press.

Tirosh-Samuelson, Hava. 2002. *Judaism and Ecology: Created World and Revealed Word*. Cambridge, MA: Harvard University Press.

White, Lynn Townsend, Jr. 1967. "The Historical Roots of Our Ecologic Crisis." *Science* 155 (1967): 1203–207.

White, Lynn Townsend, Jr. 1971. *Dynamo and Virgin Reconsidered: Essays in the Dynamism of Western Culture.* Cambridge, MA: MIT Press.

Wood, Richard L. 2002. *Faith in Action.* Chicago: University of Chicago Press.

World Wildlife Fund. 1986. *The Assisi Declarations: Messages on Man & Nature from Buddhism, Christianity, Hinduism, Islam and Judaism.* Gland, Switzerland: World Wildlife Fund.

Chronology

1950–1970—The environmental movement emerges from the conservationist movement.

1955(–)—Pierre Teilhard de Chardin's *The Phenomenon of Man* is published. In subsequent years, it becomes an influential work in conservation ecology and ecotheology.

1960–1980—Buddhist monks protecting forests in Viet Nam and Thailand become known as "conservation monks."

1960s—Ecotheology becomes a distinct branch of theology.

1966—Seyyed Hossein Nasr, professor of Islamic Studies and Islamic philosopher, addresses the ecological crisis as the spiritual crisis of modern humankind in a seminal series of University of Chicago lectures.

1967—"The Historical Roots of Our Ecologic Crisis," by Lynn Townsend White Jr., is published.

1970s—The concept *food security* is introduced in international discussions of global food supplies, food prices, food availability, and interreligious conflict.

Ecofeminist thought and writing begins influencing environmentalism.

1974—The World Council of Churches (WCC) is one of the first religious organizations to discuss environmental sustainability at the WCC Church and Society Conference on Science and Technology for Human Development.

1979—Pope John Paul II names Francis of Assisi (ca. 1181–1226) the patron saint of ecology, which formalized the general public perception of Francis as a religious environmentalist.

James Lovelock publishes the first edition of *Gaia: A New Look at Life on Earth*, which introduces the Gaia hypothesis to a broad audience.

1986—The Alliance of Religions and Conservation (ARC) is founded in collaboration with the World Wildlife Fund International (WWF).

The Assisi Declarations are written by world religious leaders and published by ARC and WWF.

1987—The United Church of Christ (UCC) publishes its *Toxic Wastes and Race Report.* The report draws attention to environmental justice in the United States and concludes that hazardous waste sites are much more likely to be located in areas where racial minorities live.

The World Council of Churches (WCC) convenes meetings in Amsterdam to discuss the ecological crisis and invites James Lovelock to discuss the Gaia hypothesis with attending theologians and religious leaders.

1988—Shomrei Adamah, Keepers of the Earth is founded, with an emphasis on educating Jewish communities about Jewish environmentalism.

1989—Buddhist monks begin ordaining trees in Thailand in an effort to resist deforestation.

1990s—The religious environmental movement emerges globally, with roots in the secular environmental movement.

1991—Bartholomew I of Constantinople organizes "Living in the Creation of the Lord," an international conference that launches the Orthodox Christian Church's environmental initiative.

1993—The National Religious Partnership on the Environment (NRPE), a U.S. interreligious collaboration, is founded.

1994—The Islamic Foundation for Ecology and Environmental Sciences (IFEES) is founded in England by Fazlun Khalid.

1995—The Evangelical Environmental Network (EEN) organizes evangelical Christians to save the United States Endangered Species Act (ESA).

1997—Interfaith Power and Light (IPL) is founded by Rev. Sally Bingham and Episcopalians, in California, United States.

1999—A Rocha Kenya (ARK), focused on marine conservation, is founded as an interdenominational Christian organization and registered as a nongovernmental environmental organization in Kenya.

2004—Prominent scientists and religious leaders issue "Earth's Climate Embraces Us All: A Plea from Religion and Science for Action on Global Climate Change," which requested that the U.S. Congress take immediate action on proposed climate change legislation.

2006—Daoist spiritual leaders in China wrote the Qinling Agreement, which pledged Daoist commitment to protecting the environment and created the Daoist Ecological Protection Network (DEPN).

The Evangelical Environmental Network (EEN) launches the Evangelical Climate Change Initiative to address climate change policy and raise climate change awareness in the United States.

2009—Hindu spiritual and religious leaders submit the first Hindu Declaration on Climate Change, at the Parliament of the World's Religions.

2010—EcoSikh is founded to disseminate knowledge about environmental issues and to help Sikh communities around the world engage in environmental activism.

2011—Bron Taylor proposes and tests the greening of religion hypothesis (GRH), which states that the world's religions are increasingly involved in environmentalism.

2014—Jinja Honcho (Association of Shinto Shrines) and the Alliance of Religions and Conservation (ARC) sponsor an international conference titled "Tradition for the Future: Culture, Faith, and Values for a Sustainable Planet," at the sacred shrine of Ise.

Thich Nhat Hanh and the 14th Dalai Lama submit Buddhist positions to the United Nations Framework Convention on Climate Change (UNFCCC), in preparation for the 2015 UNFCCC Paris Agreement on Climate Change.

2015—The Islamic Declaration on Global Climate Change is drafted at the International Islamic Climate Change Symposium and made available to all Muslims and the general public.

The Hindu Declaration on Climate Change is submitted to the United Nations Framework Convention on Climate Change (UNFCCC), in preparation for the 2016 Paris Agreement.

Pope Francis I releases the papal encyclical *Laudato Si': On Care for Our Common Home*, which is the Roman Catholic Church's first encyclical on the natural environment.

2016—The Religion and Conservation Biology Working Group of the Society for Conservation Biology (RCBWG), in collaboration with the International Marine Conservation Congress, publishes *Best Practices Guidelines for Interacting with Faith-Based Leaders and Communities.*

The International Network of Engaged Buddhists (INEB) and their Interfaith Climate and Ecology network (ICE) launch the Eco-Temple Community Development Project, with initiatives in India, Myanmar, Thailand, Japan, China, and South Korea.

In March, an international group of religious leaders submit to the UN the Interfaith Climate Change Statement to World Leaders, in support of the Paris Agreement.

In April, the 2015 draft of the Paris Agreement on Climate Change is signed by a majority of UN member nations.

2017—The UN begins the Faith for Earth initiative, which works with religious organizations to achieve the UN Sustainable Development Goals (SDGs) set for 2030.

Interfaith Power and Light (IPL) initiates their "Paris: We're Still In" campaign in response to the United States withdrawing from the United Nations' Paris Agreement on Climate Change.

The Religious Action Center of Reform Judaism (RAC) publishes its Resolution on Addressing the Impacts of Climate Change, in which Reform Judaism encourages congregations to take political action to "uphold or go beyond the commitments of the Paris Climate Agreement."

2019—The Catholic Church's Pontifical Academy of Science sponsors an international conference on biodiversity, ecosystems, and species protection, followed by the formal statement, Science and Actions for Species Protection: Noah's Arks for the 21st Century, which urges social changes to protect biodiversity.

The Religious Action Center of Reform Judaism (RAC) announces formal political support for the Green New Deal.

A

Alliance of Religions and Conservation

The Alliance of Religions and Conservation (ARC) was a secular organization based in the United Kingdom that provided support from 1986 to 2019 for religious groups that were interested in conservation and environmentalism. The idea for ARC began in 1986, when Prince Philip, who was the president of World Wildlife Fund (WWF) International, invited religious leaders from Buddhism, Christianity, Hinduism, Islam, and Judaism to attend a special WWF meeting in Assisi, Italy, on religion's role in environmental conservation. Out of this meeting came both the Assisi Declarations, in 1986, and the eventual creation of the Alliance of Religions and Conservation, in 1995. The mission of ARC was to facilitate cooperation among religious organizations and environmental organizations around the world, as well as to assist in the development of new, faith-based conservation programs. Additionally, ARC provided funds that supported faith-based conservation programs, and it published materials on religion, conservation, and ARC initiatives. According to ARC, religions are in a position to lead conservation efforts locally, regionally, and globally, because many people seek guidance on environmental issues from religious leaders. In the twenty-first century, ARC's projects involved several religious traditions including the Baha'i faith, Buddhism, Christianity, Confucianism, Daoism, Hinduism, Islam, Jainism, Judaism, Shinto, Sikhism, and Zoroastrianism.

ARC's projects ranged from local to global in scope, with financial networks, political leaders, and world organizations such as the United Nations and World Bank providing support as secular financial partners. Examples of local or regional ARC projects included eco-coffin projects in South Africa; protecting sacred Shinto forests in Japan; conservation of rare sacred orchids in Mexico; restoring an ancient Christian rock shrine in

1

England; and setting up Saudi Arabia's first biosphere reserve. ARC also encouraged religious communities to become actively involved in promoting conservation through land use practices, education, media outreach, lifestyle choices, and issue advocacy. ARC was involved in numerous international and global projects, such as the Green Pilgrimage Network (GPN), Mapping Sacred Forests, and the FaithInvest Network, which provided investment opportunities aligned with religious values. Although ARC created financial online platforms such as FaithInvest for institutional use, in all ARC projects, the primary, stated goal was to assist local communities that were interested in applying their religious values to conservation efforts.

ARC emerged in response to needs not being met by national governments or other secular political bodies. ARC defined itself as a secular organization and only accepted funds from secular sources such as the World Bank, the United Nations, and national governments. Acting as an intermediary, ARC would then assign those funds and resources only to projects developed by religious communities. In June 2019 ARC formally closed after twenty-three years of working with the world's major religions and environmental organizations. For decades, ARC had provided a bridge between religious and secular environmental efforts and had increased cooperation among people of different religious traditions who were concerned about environmental issues. Some of ARC's projects involved politically contentious issues as well as cooperation across political and social boundaries. Because of its projects, use of long-term strategies, and alliances with political leaders, ARC continues to be remembered for having encouraged religious communities to become politically engaged with environmental policy both locally and across national boundaries.

See also: Assisi Declarations; Green Pilgrimage Network

Further Reading

Palmer, Martin. 2003. *Faith in Conservation: New Approaches to Religions and the Environment*. Directions in Development Series. Washington, DC: World Bank.

Rinpoche, Lungrig, L. Serrini, K. Singh, O. Naseef, and A. Hertzberg. 1986. *The Assisi Declarations: Messages on Man and Nature from Buddhism, Christianity, Hinduism, Islam and Judaism*. Bath, UK: Alliance of Religions and Conservation.

Animism

Animism refers to the belief that all objects, phenomena, and life-forms have a spirit or soul or are inhabited by living energy. The term was introduced into anthropology in 1871 by E. B. Tylor, who theorized that the earliest form of religious belief was the attribution of spirits or souls to natural phenomena and inanimate objects. Tylor asserted that this belief was an attempt by humans to explain the causes of sleep, dreams, trances, death, and the images experienced in dreams and trances. *Animism* is also used to refer to a type of religion or belief system that asserts a life-force exists in all things and phenomena, all of which are believed to be interrelated. Some practitioners of animism believe in energy rather than spirits or supernatural entities, and variations of animism have been incorporated into contemporary Paganism, New Age beliefs, and religions that historically have been hostile to animism, such as Christianity.

Animism is an aspect commonly discussed in research that documents the motives of religiously motivated environmentalists, some of whom believe that all things in the natural world are interconnected and imbued with a shared life-force or energy. People who identify as animists typically recognize a spiritual essence or energy force in animals, plants, geological features, weather, fire, water, ancestors, or a range of other objects and phenomena. Some religions and religious adherents still resist the idea of animism and assert that spirits in general are unholy, counter to religious doctrine, or associated with demonic forces. However, many contemporary theologians and religious thinkers have used the term to explain the moral obligation of humans to recognize kinship with all of creation. Christian animism has been used to explain the natural world as having a spiritual presence, imbued with sacred power, and being animated by the Holy Spirit as part of God's creation. Similarly, in contemporary Islam, there are prominent religious scholars that discuss animism in the context of the Qur'an, arguing that there is a spiritual presence in the natural world that interacts with humans and provides opportunities for the contemplation of God's divine wisdom.

Although many religiously motivated environmentalists ground their politics in their beliefs, members of folk religions, including Indigenous communities and contemporary Pagans, are most likely to base their political actions in some form of animistic belief. Many Pagans, including Druids, Wiccans, and members of folk religions self-identify as animists; they see all of nature and inhabitants of the earth as their kin and believe that, as such, they should be protected. This may include protecting sacred animals, stones, forests, or bodies of water, which are all seen as having an energy or spirit that gives them spiritual equality with humans. Those Pagans who specifically identify as Eco-Pagans practice a type of animism that includes a commitment to environmental activism and therefore protest against injustice and cruelty to any living things, natural objects, and natural places. Eco-Pagans also participate in direct action protests, such as physically blocking construction sites, disrupting road building, or any development that may damage the natural environment.

See also: Folk Religions; Nature Religions; New Age Movement; Paganism

Further Reading

Harvey, Graham. 2006. *Animism: Respecting the Living World.* New York: Columbia University Press.

Assisi Declarations

The Assisi Declarations: Messages on Humanity and Nature from Buddhism, Christianity, Hinduism, Islam and Judaism is a document written by leaders of five major world religions and published by the World Wildlife Fund (WWF) in 1986. These religious leaders had been invited to the 1986 WWF meeting in Assisi, Italy, to discuss the role of religion in protecting and saving the natural world from environmental crisis. Assisi, Italy, had been chosen as the meeting's location because it was the birthplace of Francis of Assisi, the Catholic saint of ecology, who is known in many cultures and religious traditions for his deep love of the natural world. Secular environmentalists, religious leaders, and political leaders attended the 1986 WWF Assisi meeting, which led not only to the publication of the Declarations but also to the development of the Alliance of Religions and Conservation (ARC) as well as increased media and public interest in the WWF. In the Assisi Declarations, the leaders from the five contributing religions outline their own respective tradition's distinct approach to ecology, environmentalism, and care for the natural world. In 1995, when the Alliance of Religions and Conservation

(ARC) was formally registered as an organization, its new members from the Baha'i, Jain, Daoist, and Sikh religious traditions added statements similar to those made by the original five contributors to the Assisi Declarations.

The Buddhist section of the Assisi Declarations was written by Venerable Lungrig Namgyal Rinpoche, Abbot of Gyuto Tantric University in the 1980s, who begins with a statement on karma by the Buddha that provides the foundation for the Buddhist statement as a whole: "Because the cause was there the consequences followed; because the cause is there, the effects will follow." Rinpoche emphasizes that Buddhism is a "religion of love, understanding and compassion" committed to nonviolence and the protection of the natural environment. He explains this protection should be extended to all beings, including those "other than human" that cannot communicate their feelings, even though many humans have not protected other beings in the past.

Rinpoche is critical of those who value wildlife and other animals only in terms of their usefulness to humans, and notes that in Buddhist thought, all beings in the universe are related through the continuous cycle of birth and rebirth, just as parents and children are related. Rinpoche concludes the statement with an extensive quote by the Dalai Lama, including the assertions that "destruction of the environment and the life depending upon it is a result of ignorance, greed and disregard for the richness of all living things" and that there "is a great danger that future generations will not know the natural habitat of animals; they may not know the forests and the animals which we of this generation know to be in danger of extinction." The Buddhist statement clearly calls on this generation to take immediate action to protect the natural environment and its interdependent relations and ecosystems.

Father Lanfranco Serrini, minister general of the Franciscan Order of Friars Minor (OFM) from 1984 to 1996, introduces the Christian section of the Assisi Declarations with excerpts from Psalm 128 of the Old Testament: "Praise the Lord. . . . Praise him, sun and moon, praise him, all you shining stars! For he commanded and they were created. . . . Praise the Lord from the earth, you sea monsters and all deeps, fire and hail, snow and frost, stormy wind fulfilling his commands!" These excerpts from Psalm 128, especially relevant to the Franciscans, who model their Christianity on the work and thought of Francis of Assisi, provide the structure for Serrini's statement as a whole. Serrini explains that in praising God for God's creation, Christians show their gratitude and affirm that God made all things "visible and invisible" in the universe.

In the Christian perspective presented by Serrini, all living things and elements of the natural environment are created by God, and their purpose is to interdependently "bring to perfection the beauty of the universe" and "give glory to the Creator." Serrini also clarifies the responsibility of humans regarding the natural environment and states that "humanity's dominion cannot be understood as license to abuse, spoil, squander or destroy what God has made to manifest his glory. That dominion cannot be anything other than a stewardship in symbiosis with all creatures." Serrini concludes by declaring that contemporary Christians call for the repudiation of all "ill-considered exploitation of nature which threatens to destroy it and, in turn, to make humanity the victim of degradation."

The Hindu section of the Assisi Declarations, written by Dr. Karan Singh, president of the Hindu Virat Samaj in the 1980s, begins by referencing the Vedas, the sacred texts that contain Hindu wisdom. In the Vedas, all living and nonliving things in the universe are permeated by the same spiritual force. Singh notes that in Hinduism, although humans are at the "top of the evolutionary pyramid," they are also interconnected with the earth and all life-forms. To exemplify Hindu environmental values, Singh incorporates a sacred hymn to the earth from the *Artha Veda*, which describes Earth as a mother who provides for all of creation through her waters.

Singh also references other sacred texts, including the Upanishads and Puranas, to demonstrate that the Hindu perspective is "permeated by a reverence for life and an awareness that the great forces of nature . . . are all bound to each other within the great rhythms of nature." Singh suggests that the Hindu tradition of reverence for all forms of life should be reintroduced into contemporary society and warns that human exploitation of the environment has "finally caught up with us and a radically changed attitude towards nature is now not a question of spiritual merit or condescension, but of sheer survival." The Hindu section concludes with the ancient Hindu adage that "the Earth is our mother and we are all her children."

Representing the perspective of Muslims, Dr. Abdullah Omar Naseef, secretary general of the Muslim World League from 1983 to 1993, begins by stating that the "essence of Islamic teaching is that the entire universe is Allah's creation." Naseef enumerates the acts of Allah as creator, acknowledges the supremacy of the will of Allah in all things, and explains that for "the Muslim, mankind's role on earth is that of a Khalifah—vicegerent or trustee of Allah." Humans are meant to be "Allah's stewards" of the earth and not its masters or its owners. Naseef emphasizes that as *khalifahs* of Allah, Muslims and all humans are responsible for their actions and must be accountable for all abuses and uses of the earth.

The concept of *tawhid* is central to Islam and to Muslims' view of the natural world, and Naseef explains that tawhid, as the unity of Allah, is reflected in the "unity of man and nature." Unity (*tawhid*), trusteeship (*khalifah*), and accountability (*akhirah*) are identified as the "three central concepts of Islam" and "also the pillars of the environmental ethics of Islam." Naseef emphasizes that these pillars should guide all interaction between humans and the natural environment, including the work of scientists, technologists, politicians, and economists. Naseef asserts that if Muslims practice unity with nature, stewardship of Allah's creation, and accountability for the abuse and use of nature, then they "will create a caring and practical way of being, doing and knowing; a true Islamic alternative to the environmentally destructive thought and actions which dominate the world today."

Rabbi Arthur Hertzberg, vice president of the World Jewish Congress from 1975 to 1991, wrote the section on Judaism and nature, which is the final statement in the Assisi Declarations. Hertzberg begins by stating that "whoever is merciful to all creatures is a descendant of our ancestor Abraham" and by referencing the Talmud and Hebrew Bible. Hertzberg explains that the Jewish relationship between humans and the natural world is clearly defined in Jewish sacred texts, including the scripture that notes God "took man and put him in the Garden of Eden, to tend it and guard it" (Genesis 2:15). The relationship in Judaism between humanity and nature is described by Hertzberg as "a seamless web with humanity as the leader and custodian of the natural world." He also explains that the Jewish people, as stewards, must prioritize the protection of the natural world, and that Judaism must move collectively toward vegetarianism as "the ultimate mean of the Jewish moral teaching." Hertzberg concludes the section on the Jewish perspective by noting that "we are all passengers together in this same fragile and glorious world. Let us safeguard our rowboat—and let us row together."

See also: Alliance of Religions and Conservation; Buddhism; Christianity; Dalai Lama; Francis of Assisi; Hinduism; Islam; Judaism

Further Reading

Palmer, Martin, and Victoria Finlay. 2013. *Faith in Conservation: New Approaches to Religions and the Environment*. Washington, DC: World Bank.

World Wildlife Fund. 1986. *The Assisi Declarations: Messages on Man & Nature from Buddhism, Christianity, Hinduism, Islam and Judaism*. Gland, Switzerland: World Wildlife Fund.

B

Bartholomew I of Constantinople

Bartholomew I of Constantinople (1940–), born Dimitrios Arhondonis, in Turkey, has been the archbishop of Constantinople and ecumenical patriarch of the global Orthodox Christian Church since 1991. In the 1990s, he became known as the "green patriarch" for his commitment to environmental activism in his role as spiritual leader of the world's Orthodox Christians. Bartholomew has advocated extensively for Christianity's active participation in global environmentalism, has published several books that address environmental issues, and has issued numerous Orthodox Christian encyclicals on environmentalism and related topics. He has been a leader in creating global environmental summits and conferences that bring together theologians, religious leaders from diverse traditions, corporate representatives, and politicians. Bartholomew was one of the first leaders of a global religious institution and world religion to issue formal statements defining environmentalism as a spiritual responsibility, with the Dalai Lama and Pope Francis I making similar statements in subsequent years.

Although the Orthodox Christian Church had expressed concern for the natural environment in the 1980s, Bartholomew organized its first formal international initiative in 1991. This initiative began with "Living in the Creation of the Lord," a conference held in 1991 that included both religious leaders and secular organizations such the World Wildlife Fund (WWF). From 1994 to 1998, Bartholomew implemented the first Orthodox seminars on environmental awareness and action at the Theological School of Halki, in Turkey. During this time, Bartholomew was the driving force behind Orthodox international environmental symposia that hosted participants from diverse religions and scientific fields. These international symposia continued into the twenty-first century, focusing on environmental problems affecting the Danube River, the Adriatic Sea, the Amazon, the Arctic, the Mississippi River, and other regions. Bartholomew has supported environmentalism in his encyclicals and proclamations since 1992, and much of his theological writing has focused on environmentalism, including his 2012 book, *On Earth as in Heaven*.

Bartholomew is credited with continuously noting the effects of human action on the natural environment and convincing conservative religious adherents of their responsibility to rescue and protect God's creation. He continues to be known for his support of engaged religious environmentalism, his actions on behalf of ecumenism and diversity of religion, and his collegial responses to his critics on these and other issues. In his efforts to foster international cooperation on environmental issues, he has worked with numerous governments and global organizations, such as the United Nations. His environmentalism is based on his reading of Christian sacred texts and his conviction that "to commit a crime against the natural world is a sin . . . to cause species to become extinct and to destroy the biological diversity of God's creation . . . to degrade the integrity of the earth by causing changes in its climate—all of these are sins." Bartholomew's collaboration with Pope Francis I for the 2017 World Day of Prayer for Creation is an example of his continued ecumenical approach to environmentalism.

See also: Christianity; Dalai Lama; Pope Francis I

Further Reading

Bartholomew I, Ecumenical Patriarch of Constantinople, and John Chryssavgis. 2012. *On Earth as in Heaven: Ecological Vision and Initiatives of Ecumenical Patriarch Bartholomew*. Orthodox Christianity and Contemporary Thought. New York: Fordham University Press.

Biodiversity

Biodiversity is the genetic, species, and ecosystems diversity within a given region, including microorganisms, plants, and animals. On Earth, biodiversity is greater in regions with warm climates, such as near the equator, in tropical zones, and in the western Pacific coastal waters. Biodiversity is essential to human society and other life, providing a source of food, medicine, and raw materials. Additionally, those ecosystems with rich biodiversity provide a higher quality of natural ecosystem services, such as cleaning the air and water, that are essential to all life-forms. Ecosystems with rich biodiversity are also more resilient against floods, fires, and other extreme disturbances. Threats to biodiversity include habitat destruction, deforestation, climate change, pollution, and overpopulation, as well as overexploitation and decreases in genetic diversity, with human activity being a primary cause of many of these threats. Habitat destruction and deforestation are often the result of human activity, such urbanization, conversion of forests into ranch or farmland, or drilling and mining operations. Human activity also results in anthropogenic climate change, pollution, and overharvesting food and other resources from forests, oceans, or other ecosystems. The environmental pressures caused by the planet's human population, estimated at 7.7 billion in 2019, have resulted in loss of animal and plant species. Most scientists assert that this decrease in biodiversity has diminished the earth's ability to supply clear air and water, rich soil, and food sources.

Although most religious traditions have just recently begun making formal statements about biodiversity, their ability to shape people's beliefs and values on environmental issues has been noted by many scholars and scientists for several decades. A majority of the world's population belongs to a religious tradition, which provides followers with a moral code, a cosmology, and strategies for interacting with other species and the natural environment. Although religions vary in their beliefs regarding other species and the natural environment, in general, most religions support preservation and protection of biodiversity, which they view as part of a divine creation. Religious beliefs and practices often include the protection of sacred lands, rivers, forests, mountains, plants, or animals, and include taboos, distinctions between respectful and disrespectful behavior, and regulation of interactions with different species.

Several researchers have noted that religious practices, which develop over centuries, often involve the sustainable use of natural resources, such as regional plants, wildlife, and even domesticated animals. Although biodiversity is usually not the stated intent of these practices, it is often the outcome and is facilitated through traditional ecological knowledge (TEK) or traditions rooted in ancient sacred texts. Since religions are known to shape attitudes and lifestyles, and religious adherents are living in regions in which biodiversity is at risk, researchers have urged conservation scientists to include religions in their discussions about biodiversity. Responding to these recommendations and the urgency of biodiversity loss, many global organizations, environmentalists, scientists, and representatives of religious traditions increasingly collaborate on biodiversity issues.

In the first decades of the twenty-first century, a great deal of progress was made toward strengthening collaborations among religious traditions, scientists, governments, and financial entities such as banks or corporations. In 2019 for instance, in response to a recent report by the Intergovernmental Science-Policy Platform on Biodiversity and Ecosystem Services (IPBES), the Catholic Church's Pontifical Academy of Science sponsored an international conference on biodiversity, ecosystems, and species protection. The IPBES had studied biodiversity for several years and concluded that 25 percent of Earth's animal and plant species will be extinct within decades if changes are not implemented. The conference participants, including representatives from natural history museums, botanical gardens, zoos, aquariums, and experts in biodiversity and ecology, discussed the anthropogenic factors causing the decline in biodiversity, such as deforestation, climate change, land use, overfishing, and pollution.

Following the 2019 conference, the Pontifical Academy of Science and the conference participants released a formal statement titled "Science and Actions for Species Protection: Noah's Arks for the 21st Century," in which they call for conservationist leaders, scientists, policy advisers, and religious communities around the world to build an improved and sustainable relationship with the natural environment and its millions of species. In the statement, the conference participants admitted "that attempts to build 'Noah's Arks for the 21st century' will not be sufficient" because "fundamental societal change is needed." In the statement they list fossil fuel consumption, food waste, land-use change, and deforestation as the "fundamental drivers of climate change leading to biodiversity losses and species extinctions."

In addition to institutional networking among formally appointed religious leaders, scientists, and policy advisers, many religiously motivated environmentalists take an activist approach to biodiversity. Vandana Shiva, a globally recognized expert on biodiversity, is one of the numerous examples of religiously motivated activism. Hinduism and sacred Vedic texts are the source of Shiva's belief that biodiversity is a sacred gift that includes soil, seeds, and all life-forms. Much of Shiva's activism and research focus on supporting food systems based on biodiversity that nourish the web of life, as well as eliminating food systems based on greed and ignorance that lead to loss of biodiversity and the collapse of ecosystems.

In support of biodiversity, Shiva has researched and presented on the issue globally and has also initiated community projects that include farmers' religious beliefs, sustainability, and biodiversity in agricultural practices. Shiva asserts that biodiversity of seeds, soils, and ecosystems in general are essential to all life and that corporate agriculture threatens this biodiversity, while local communities strengthen biodiversity through their agricultural practices. She is an advocate for an "Earth democracy" based on biodiversity and cultural diversity and has led campaigns against genetic engineering of foods, food patents, and seed patents, all of which threaten biodiversity in the natural environment. Shiva's activism for biodiversity is rooted in her Hindu religious tradition, including practicing the Hindu belief of dharma, which refers to sustainable living in relation with all things interconnected in the universe's web of life.

In addition to leaders of the world's religions and religiously motivated activists, there are several formal global networks dedicated to biodiversity that emphasize the importance of spirituality and religion. The International Union for Conservation of Nature (IUCN), the largest and most diverse of these global networks, provides a "neutral forum in which governments, NGOs, scientists, businesses, local communities, Indigenous peoples groups, faith-based organizations and others can work together to forge and implement solutions to environmental challenges." In 1998 the World Commission on Protected Areas (WCPA), one of IUCN's subdivisions, established the Cultural and Spiritual Values Specialist Group (CSVPA) to research cultural and spiritual values that promote biodiversity and environmentalism. CSVPA's current biodiversity initiatives include the Delos Initiative, which works to maintain the biodiversity and sanctity of sacred natural sites in developed countries, and the Sacred Natural Site Initiative (SNSI), which works with the guardians of sacred natural sites around the world to protect, conserve, revitalize, and promote these sites.

CSVPA has generated and collected numerous case studies that provide guidelines for integrating the spiritual significance of nature and biodiversity into conservation strategies, governance arrangements, management and planning, and tourism development. A few recent examples of these case studies on biodiversity, religion, and spirituality include Protecting Sacred Maya Caves, in Yucatan, Mexico (Maya); Cultural and Spiritual Significance of Nature in Interpretation, Management, and

Governance at Great Smoky Mountains National Park, United States (Cherokee); and the Cultural Monastic Landscape of Vanatori Neamt Nature Park, Romania (Orthodox Christianity). The work of CSVPA is representative of the increased collaboration on biodiversity issues over the last few decades between religions, spiritual traditions, governments, scientists, and economic institutions.

See also: Climate Change; Deforestation; Overpopulation; Pollution; Shiva, Vandana

Further Reading

Negi, Chandra S. 2014. *The Sacred Uttarakhand: Ethno-Biological Study Surrounding Sacred Natural Sites in Uttarakhand.* Dehra Dun, India: Bishen Singh Mahendra Pal Singh.

O'Brien, Kevin J. 2010. *An Ethics of Biodiversity: Christianity, Ecology, and the Variety of Life.* Washington, DC: Georgetown University Press.

Pontifical Academy of Science. 2019. *Final Statement, Science and Actions for Species Protection: Noah's Arks for the 21st Century.* Vatican City: Pontifical Academy of Science.

Pungetti, Gloria, Gonzalo Oviedo, and Della Hooke. 2012. *Sacred Species and Sites: Advances in Biocultural Conservation.* Cambridge, UK: Cambridge University Press.

Verschuuren, Bas, and Steve Brown, eds. 2019. *Cultural and Spiritual Significance of Nature in Protected Areas: Governance, Management and Policy.* Abingdon, UK: Routledge.

Buddhism

Buddhism is a religion and spiritual path with roots in the ancient Vedic tradition and the Sramana movements of India that eventually rejected the authority of the Brahmin priests and ritualism of Hinduism. Gautama Buddha, the founder of Buddhism, lived between 500 and 350 BCE in Nepal and the northern regions of India. Although he was a prince from an elite family, at age twenty-nine Gautama Buddha began a spiritual awakening that led him to reject his wealth and status to become a wandering ascetic seeking and teaching the path to enlightenment. His teachings and sayings were passed down orally by followers and eventually written down in 80 BCE in the Pali Canon, which includes the words and teachings of both

Buddha and his disciples. As Buddhism spread, it developed several traditions, including the two major branches of Theravada and Mahayana, which share the core beliefs found in the Four Noble Truths, the Eightfold Path, the cycle of rebirth driven by karma (samsara), and the Five Precepts. Some Buddhist traditions believe in many deities, some believe Gautama Buddha is a deity, and some believe there are no deities, but Buddhism in general does not teach that there is one supreme god responsible for creation. The belief in karma and the cycle of rebirth, however, continues to be universal throughout modern Buddhism. In 2015 the Buddhist population was estimated at more than 520 million adherents, with a majority living in the Asia and Pacific regions and the remainder in communities around the world.

Although contemporary Buddhist environmentalism is based in the original teachings of Buddha, he did not provide specific, distinct teachings on the relationship between humans and the natural environment. However, Buddha's teachings, including the Four Noble Truths, Noble Eightfold Path, the Five Precepts, and belief in the interconnection of all life through karma and rebirth, all suggest that ethical behavior includes compassion toward all life and the sustainable use of resources. Buddha taught that the Noble Eightfold Path, or Middle Way, ends suffering through right understanding, right thought, right speech, right action, right livelihood, right effort, right mindfulness, and right concentration. In the Five Precepts, Buddha provides the guidelines for ethical human conduct: do not harm any living creature; do not steal, and be generous in giving; do not take more than you need; do not lie; and do not act thoughtlessly.

Individuals seeking spiritual enlightenment should follow the Five Precepts by not harming any living creature, using resources only as needed, and using both the Eightfold Path and the Five Precepts as guides for ethical thought and action. Some of Buddha's teachings provide explicit guidance for human interaction with the natural world, such as the necessity of love and nonviolence, not harming others, and avoiding professions that harm others or kill animals. Additionally, some beliefs in Buddhism, such as the belief that karma and the cycle of rebirth are essential for spiritual enlightenment, have traditionally shaped Buddhist views of the natural environment. Although Buddhism has been described as more environmentalist than some religions, Buddhist teachings that specifically address environmental issues actually originate with modern Buddhist activists, scholars, or teachers.

Buddhist scholars note that ancient Buddhist texts view the material world as a transient or impermanent condition from which individuals should seek to be liberated, while conversely many contemporary Buddhists see political engagement with the material world as one way to seek the truth, create positive karma, and pursue enlightenment. Although a few Buddhist leaders and communities recognized the threat of industrialism to the natural environment as early as the beginning of the twentieth century, organized political engagement of environmental issues did not occur in Buddhism until the 1960s. As the strategies and tactics of the secular environmental movement began spreading around the world, many Buddhist communities began developing a distinctly Buddhist approach to environmentalism.

In the 1970s, for example, Buddhist conservation monks in Thailand were formally organizing to protect forests from multinational corporate logging, and the engaged Buddhism approach began merging ancient Buddhist practices with social action and activism. Since then, engaged Buddhism approaches that focus on environmentalism have taken several forms globally, including green Buddhism, eco-Dharma, and eco-Buddhism. In the twenty-first century, the internet, social media, and other advances in technology have contributed to the emergence of an international Buddhism that draws inspiration from several different contemporary teachers and encourages political engagement at the local, regional, and global levels. Although ancient Buddhist texts teach the interdependence of all life and respect for the natural world, it was relatively recently that the secular environmental movement and engaged Buddhism led to a distinctly Buddhist environmentalism.

In the 1960s Vietnamese Buddhist teacher Thich Nhat Hanh introduced the concept of engaged Buddhism as a way to connect meditation and Buddhist teachings to the many struggles in society, including environmental issues, social justice, poverty, and political conflict. Since then, engaged Buddhism has become a distinct path that grounds social action, including environmentalism, in Buddhist teachings and asserts that the Four Truths, Eightfold Path, and Five Precepts encourage nonviolent activism as an enlightened response to the suffering in the world and as a way to build a sustainable and compassionate world. "Inter-being" is a core concept in engaged Buddhism and is based on the Buddhist principle of dependent origination (*pratityasamutpada*) that defines all beings and phenomena as interdependent and arising from multiple causes and conditions. Through inter-being, all beings are interconnected elements of the natural environment that, if destroyed or degraded, will cause suffering for all humanity.

When considering environmental issues, adherents of engaged Buddhism believe they should meditate to obtain insight and then engage in social activism as a path to self-transformation and social transformation. Engaged Buddhism also emphasizes that nonviolent environmental activism, informed by meditation and Buddhist teachings, should be combined with a commitment to social justice and democracy. Compassion and loving-kindness are also core concepts of engaged Buddhism, and both are considered essential elements of environmental activism. On the path to enlightenment through environmental activism, a person is expected to act with compassion and love toward all species at all times. In engaged Buddhism, this compassion includes protecting biodiversity, avoiding harmful treatment of all sentient beings, promoting sustainability, resisting actions that have negative effects on the natural environment, and working collectively to address all ecological threats.

Deforestation, often occurring near rural communities engaged in subsistence agriculture, is an example of an issue being addressed by communities following engaged Buddhism practices. In the late 1980s, Buddhist conservation monks in Thailand began ordaining trees, a ritual that included reciting verses from the Pali Canon, clothing the trees in monk's robes, and reading from Buddhist texts that discuss enlightenment, karma and rebirth, the interrelatedness of all life, the alleviation of suffering, and conservation. The tree ordination ceremonies included both Buddhist monks and rural communities, with the goals of resisting destructive logging and corporate predatory lending practices that were contributing to loss of forests and woodland ecosystems. These Buddhist monks focused on community forest rights for Indigenous people and subsistence farmers but for years were often persecuted or even assassinated for their activism, which challenged the appropriation of forests and woodlands by the Thai government, logging companies, corporate farming, and oil companies.

By the late 1990s, nongovernmental agencies such as the International Network of Engaged Buddhists (INEB), WWF-Thailand, and the Alliance of Religions and Conservation (ARC) were working with Thailand's ecology monks and rural communities. Ecology monks, also known as conservation monks, often have advanced education in the natural and social sciences, which helps them participate in the political sphere on behalf of rural villagers and subsistence farmers. Ecology monks practicing engaged Buddhism have recently begun tree ordination in Cambodia, which is experiencing similar environmental issues to those in Thailand brought on by unsustainable corporate development. In these and other countries in Asia, ecology monks practicing engaged Buddhism are helping Buddhists frame environmentalism as a moral duty and further understand the connections between deforestation, devasting floods, soil depletion, climate change, displacement of subsistence farmers, and unsustainable development.

Started in 2016 by the International Network of Engaged Buddhists (INEB) and their Interfaith Climate and Ecology network (ICE), the Eco-Temple Community Development Project is recent example of engaged Buddhism applied to environmentalist concerns. INEB created a model of Buddhist environmentalism based on the Four Noble Truths that teach about the existence of suffering, the cause of suffering, the end of suffering, and the path that leads to that end. INEB members view their environmental activities over the years, which include discovering the structural, cultural, and political causes of environmental degradation, as part of a distinctly Buddhist approach tied to discovering the cause of suffering. By creating a model of environmentally sustainable communities, INEB members believe they offer a Buddhist vision of society that ends suffering due to environmental issues, as opposed to the current models of development that are degrading the natural environment. Finally, INEB members design and implement activities, such as the Eco-Temple Project, that provide the means to achieve an alternate vision of society that is sustainable and protects the natural environment, thereby presenting a path that leads to the end of suffering.

INEB is especially concerned about suffering in Asia associated with environmental degradation, such as deforestation for corporate farming or massive dams built to power industrialization, and Eco-Temple sites have been established in India, Myanmar, Thailand, Japan, China, and South Korea. These Eco-Temples are created on the following principles: ecological temple structure and energy system; economic sustainability; integration with surrounding environment; engagement with community and other regional groups; and development of spiritual values and teachings on environment. The designing and building of an Eco-Temple represent a collaborative effort among rural communities, Buddhists, religious leaders, and political leaders.

At the international level, Buddhists have made formal statements on several environmental issues and worked with global organizations such as the United Nations. Thich Nhat Hanh, who began teaching engaged Buddhism in the 1960s and continues to be a global force in Buddhism, has made several formal public statements on environmental issues. One of his recent statements, *Falling in Love with the Earth*, was written in response to a request in 2014 from the United Nations Framework Convention on Climate Change (UNFCCC) in preparation for the UNFCCC Paris Agreement. Thich Nhat Hanh states that the "Earth and all species on Earth are in real danger." He emphasizes the importance of compassion and nonviolence and warns that "much of what we drink, eat, watch, read or listen to, is toxic, polluting our bodies and minds with violence, anger, fear and despair." After noting several aspects of the global environmental crisis, Hanh notes hopefully that "our love and admiration for the Earth has the power to unite us and remove all boundaries, separation and discrimination."

The Dalai Lama, another global force in Buddhism, has written several books that include comments about environmental issues, with his statements for the 2015 Paris Agreement defining climate change as a "problem which human beings created" and urging all people to "take a more active role in protecting this planet, including the Tibetan plateau." Other Buddhists from around the world continue to respond to the requests of leaders such as the Dalai Lama and Thich Nhat Hanh, and the United Nations has added several environmental programs, such as the UN Faith For Earth Initiative launched in 2017 that works with religious organizations to achieve the UN Sustainable Development Goals (SDGs) set for 2030.

See also: Alliance of Religions and Conservation; Dalai Lama; Environmental Justice; Paris Agreement; Religious Environmental Movement

Further Reading

Bstan-'dzin-rgya-mtsho Dalai Lama XIV. 2018. *Ecology, Ethics, and Interdependence: The Dalai Lama in Conversation with Leading Thinkers on Climate Change*. Edited by John Anthony Dunne and Daniel Goleman. Somerville, MA: Wisdom Publications.

Darlington, Susan M. 2012. *The Ordination of a Tree: The Thai Buddhist Environmental Movement*. Albany: State University of New York Press.

James, Simon P. 2017. *Zen Buddhism and Environmental Ethics*. New York: Taylor & Francis.

Kaza, Stephanie. 2019. *Green Buddhism: Practice and Compassionate Action in Uncertain Times*. Boulder, CO: Shambhala.

Nhat Hanh Thich. 2009. *Interbeing: Fourteen Guidelines for Engaged Buddhism*. New Delhi: Full Circle.

C

Christianity

Christianity is a religion that originated more than two thousand years ago in the Roman province of Judea, located in the southern region of Palestine. Christianity teaches that Jesus of Nazareth is the Messiah and Son of God, whose coming was prophesized in the Old Testament or Hebrew Bible. Along with Judaism and Islam, Christianity is a monotheistic religion in the Abrahamic tradition. Christian belief is based on the sacred texts of the Old Testament, which is based on the Hebrew Bible, and on the New Testament, which includes the life and teachings of Jesus of Nazareth, known as Jesus Christ. Christianity is the world's largest religion, with around 2.3 billion adherents in 2015, and most of its members belong to one of four major branches: Catholicism, Protestantism, the Eastern Orthodox Church, and Oriental Orthodoxy. Although beliefs and practices vary by region, denomination, congregation, culture, and individual, Christians of all types share some fundamental beliefs. These shared beliefs, based on the Old Testament and the New Testament, include (1) Jesus Christ is the Messiah and Son of God prophesized in the Old Testament; (2) Jesus was crucified, suffered, died, entombed, and then resurrected from death; and (3) Jesus grants forgiveness of sins, salvation, and reconciliation with God.

In Christianity the relationship between humans and the natural world historically has been defined by the Old Testament's use of the word *dominion*. The scripture most commonly referenced regarding this relationship is from the book of Genesis, which states that humankind will "have dominion over the fish of the sea, and over the birds of the air, and over the cattle, and over all the wild animals of the earth, and over every creeping thing that creeps upon the earth" (Genesis 1:26). The concept of dominion has been translated and interpreted in different ways over the centuries, with other terms found in scripture such as *rule* or *subdue* also being subject to interpretation.

Although Christian scriptures emphasize that humans are made in God's image, and as such, humans should rule or hold dominion over the natural environment, Christians have not always agreed about how humans should exert dominion. In general, many contemporary scholars have suggested that the concept of dominion in Christianity has been used to justify destructive exploitation of the natural environment. However, Christian scholars and theologians tend to support a more nuanced explanation of dominion: dominion as the type of love exemplified by the shepherd tending a flock, dominion as humankind's responsibility as stewards of God's creation, or dominion as a benevolent ruler serving the common interest. Although the concept of dominion has several interpretations, these various definitions focus on the role of humans, which has led to Christianity being described as anthropocentric.

Some scholars, such as Lynn Townsend White Jr., have argued that Christianity is anthropocentric and views the natural world as existing solely to serve human needs. This argument further asserts that anthropocentrism has combined with the biblical mandate for dominion and led to destructive exploitation of the natural world. There are several recurring responses to these types of arguments about Christianity, anthropocentrism, and human interactions with the natural world. One response is that Christianity is extremely diverse, by culture, region, time period, and community or congregation, so a blanket statement that Christianity is anthropocentric, destructive, and concerned with domination over the natural world is not an accurate description. Another recurring response is that several religions, not just Christianity, have been appropriated for political or economic interests and used as a means by which to dominate, destroy, degrade, and exploit the natural world. One response offered by Christians themselves is that Christianity is theocentric, not anthropocentric, with each thing created by God finding meaning and purpose in its relationship to the Creator. The Franciscan movement, which emerged in medieval Europe, is both a historical and a contemporary example of ecological theocentrism that praises God for all things yet also sees each thing in the natural environment as a means to experience God. In the twenty-first century, Christian discussions of theocentrism increasingly claim that environmentally sustainable practices are required of humankind to fulfill its distinct purpose, which includes the biblical command to care for "the garden" of creation.

When the secular environmental movement emerged in the 1960s, it was met with mixed reactions from Christians. Although ecotheology and stewardship of nature were increasingly discussed in Christianity as early as the 1950s, these trends were not equally represented in all Christian denominations and congregations. Initially, many members of the environmental movement were critical of several social practices, lifestyles, and beliefs that they saw as connected in some way to Christianity. Criticisms of Christianity by secular environmentalists included that it was directly involved with or responsible for oppressive patriarchy, the subordination of women and Indigenous peoples, unsustainable use of natural resources, unsustainable family structures and size, irresponsible reproductive practices, and hostility toward gay people or non-heterosexual lifestyles.

Conversely, some Christians were critical of the progressive politics of environmentalists who argued for social equality regardless of lifestyle or beliefs, the liberation of women, population control and birth control, and rejection of religious authority. Whether these generalizations were accurate or not, they were indicative of a lack of trust that persisted for years between many environmentalists and Christians. It is true that Christianity as a powerful religious institution had a role in colonization, domination, oppression, and related environmental degradation over the centuries. However, it is also true that Christianity since its inception has included a wide range of beliefs and practices, some of which encourage respect for nature and sustainable use of natural resources.

Early Christianity was focused on the salvation of humanity through reconciliation with God. Early Christianity also supported the belief that the natural world had value because it was created by God and served human needs. Although there was a distinct separation between the spiritual world and the material world, in the New Testament scriptures God is actively involved in the natural world and explicitly directs the natural world to provide sustenance for his creatures. In the New Testament, nature is considered worthy of representing the divine, and Jesus often uses metaphors and parables drawn from nature. In the Gospels of Matthew, Mark, and Luke, for example, the "Parable of the Mustard Seed" compares the kingdom of God to a tiny mustard seed that becomes a large plant.

In medieval Europe, the early Christian approach to the natural world, with nature as a medium for praising God and witnessing his creation, was enhanced most notably by Francis of Assisi and the Franciscan movement. Following the Protestant Reformation in the 1500s, there have been increasingly numerous variations of the definition of Christian steward-ship. For example, some Christian communities have insisted that vegetar-ianism is the ultimate form of Christian environmental stewardship, while others believe God created animals specifically as food for humans. Similarly, some U.S. Evangelical Christians oppose secular environmen-talism, while others collaborate and cooperate with nonreligious environ-mental activists. Currently, influenced by ecotheology, ecofeminism, and the interest of their younger generations, many Evangelical Christians have become instrumental in formally redefining environmental steward-ship as "creation care" mandated by God in the Old and New Testaments.

In the twenty-first century, many Christians have embraced envir-onmentalism as part of their mission, belief system, and theology. Ecotheology, ecofeminism, secular ideas such as the Gaia hypothesis, and the work of theologian Pierre Teilhard de Chardin are just a few of the important influences on Christianity's collective decision to embrace many aspects of environmentalism. As early as the 1950s, Teilhard de Chardin and other Catholic theologians were introducing new interpretations of human relations with the natural world, including the concept of a Cosmic Christ, a noösphere or web comprised of the interacting souls of all of creation, and a shift from a hierarchical model of creation to an under-standing of all life in creation as interrelated. Catholic, Orthodox, and Protestant theologians developed theologies of nature that would emerge by the late 1960s as ecotheology, in response both to critics of Christianity and to Christians themselves asking for guidance on environmental issues.

Ecotheology continues to transform Christianity by examining Christian scripture in the context of environmental issues, with the goal of guiding human interaction with the natural world. Beginning in the 1970s, Christian ecofeminists, many influenced by ecotheology, called for Christians to examine their role in the exploitation of nature and the oppression of women, and to prioritize environmental issues as part of Christian stewardship. In the 1970s many Christian thinkers and writers were also reacting and responding to the environmentalist ideas of scien-tists, such as Lovelock's Gaia hypothesis that theorized about the interre-latedness of all things on the planet.

In addition to new approaches in theology, institutional changes related to environmentalism have also occurred in twenty-first-century Christianity. Evangelical leaders have developed, practiced, and shared the creation care model; Pope Francis I prioritized environmental issues in Catholic doctrine; and Ecumenical Patriarch Bartholomew I, of the Eastern

Orthodox church, has asserted Christians are obligated to address environmental issues. The creation care model is a biblically based approach that asserts that humans are commanded to take care of God's creation, which is understood to include the natural environment. Evangelicals have historically emphasized that true Christian belief can only be achieved by knowing the scriptures in the Old Testament and New Testament, and that this biblical authority guides all true Christian action and thought. By identifying and interpreting relevant biblical scripture, Evangelicals have come to understand that creation care is a type of religious environmentalism that is mandated by God. In the Catholic Church, Pope Francis I published the papal encyclical *Laudato Si': On Care for Our Common Home* in 2015; it references the Franciscan tradition, states the "whole human family" should be working together on environmental issues, and confirms the urgency of the planet's current environmental crisis. Similarly, Patriarch Bartholomew I of the Eastern Orthodox Church has been publicly speaking and writing since the 1990s on the importance of environmental protection, as well as creating several initiatives around the world to address specific environmental problems.

Christianity, including its major branches and numerous traditions around the world, has been developing new approaches in theology and doctrine for several decades aimed at understanding the role of Christianity in the environmental movement. Theologians, leaders, and laypersons from all major branches of Christianity eventually forged a distinct religious environmental movement, even though many Christians were initially opposed to some of the beliefs of the secular environmental movement. By the early decades of the twenty-first century, the major branches of Christianity had integrated new theological approaches into doctrine and practice, noted the environmentalist tendencies of their younger generations, developed interreligious networks and reached out to secular environmentalists, and helped advance policies addressing environmental problems such as climate change, food security, pollution, and biodiversity.

Regardless of these changes, Christianity continues to be theocentric and monotheistic, and interpretation of biblical scripture regarding environmental issues is ongoing. Collaborations among secular environmentalists, Christian environmentalists, theologians, institutional religious leaders, and scientists continue to inspire new ways for Christians to understand their role in environmentalism. For example, some Christians have borrowed the concept of reconciliation ecology from the sciences of ecology and biology, and suggest it can improve Christianity's creation care model and environmental stewardship. In Christian reconciliation ecology, humans must recognize the wrongs they committed against God's creation, show remorse regarding these wrongs, minimize further harm and repair the harm done, accept forgiveness, and then move forward in a new relationship with God and all of creation.

See also: Bartholomew I of Constantinople; Ecofeminism; Ecotheology; Evangelical Environmental Network; Francis of Assisi; Pope Francis I; Religious Environmental Movement; Teilhard de Chardin, Pierre; White, Lynn Townsend, Jr.

Further Reading

Chryssavgis, John, and Bruce V. Foltz, eds. 2013. *Toward an Ecology of Transfiguration: Orthodox Christian Perspectives on Environment, Nature, and Creation.* New York: Fordham University Press.

Lin, Johnny Wei-Bing. 2016. *The Nature of Environmental Stewardship: Understanding Creation Care Solutions to Environmental Problems.* Eugene, OR: Wipf and Stock Publishers.

Warners, David, Michael Ryskamp, and Randall Van Dragt. 2014. "Reconciliation Ecology: A New Paradigm for Advancing Creation Care." *Perspectives on Science & Christian Faith* 66 (4): 221–35.

Winright, Tobias L. 2011. *Green Discipleship: Catholic Theological Ethics and the Environment.* Winona, MN: Anselm Academic.

Climate Change

Climate change refers to significant changes in the earth's climate system, including its atmosphere, biosphere, cryosphere, hydrosphere, and lithosphere, that cause prolonged or permanent shifts in weather patterns. The effects of climate change in the twenty-first century include global temperature rise, glacial retreat and shrinking ice sheets, warming and acidification of the oceans, rising sea levels, and extreme weather. Factors that lead to climate change are called forcing mechanisms, which can be internal mechanisms, which are natural processes of climate systems, or external mechanisms, such as increased CO_2 emissions from human activity, changes in solar activity, or changes in the earth's orbit. Some external mechanisms are beyond human control, but anthropogenic factors, which are those factors created by human activity, are having the greatest impact on climate change that affects human societies and the natural environment.

In 2014 the Intergovernmental Panel on Climate Change (IPCC) confirmed the incontrovertible scientific evidence that anthropogenic factors are significantly changing and warming the climate system. The most concerning of these anthropogenic factors is increased CO_2 levels from combusting fossil fuel, with other anthropogenic factors such as particulate matter, CO_2 from manufacturing, large-scale raising of cattle for meat, and deforestation also significantly affecting the climate system. The global scientific consensus is that humans are significantly contributing to climate change that will negatively impact life on Earth, and that Earth's surface temperature will likely continue to rise in the twenty-first century, the oceans will acidify, heat waves will occur with increased frequency and endurance, and weather events will become more extreme.

Scientists have been concerned since at least the 1930s that human activity has been negatively impacting the planet's climate system. Since 2007, the IPCC has stated without reservation that Earth's climate system is warming as the "result of human activities" and primarily because of greenhouse gases. The IPCC predicts that increased concentration of these gases will result in continued rising sea levels, increased floods and drought, and coastal erosion, which are predicted to negatively impact millions of people globally. Communities in regions that are already environmentally stressed will not be able to grow adequate food and will experience increases in malnutrition, disease, and competition over essential resources. National security agencies around the world predict that degradation of natural resources combined with climate change will not only cause health issues but will increasingly trigger conflict, civil wars, and mass migrations. Scientific evidence of anthropogenic climate change is clear, and projections regarding its effects on human populations and the natural environment have been acknowledged by international organizations and most governments around the world. However, getting governments, corporations, and the public to agree on how to address climate change issues has been difficult. Many activists, scholars, global organizations, and governments believe that because of its influence on a majority of the world's population, religion has the power to help create an effective response to climate change.

In the past few decades, the accumulation of scientific evidence and the increased number of human lives being affected by climate change have forced governments, corporations, and communities to search for immediate solutions. Governments and other policy makers have struggled to agree and act on climate change responses, although there has been agreement that human lifestyles, behaviors, and use of resources need to change quickly. Religions and belief systems are increasingly recognized for their potential to mobilize people on environmental issues such as climate change and for their general ability to influence collective behavior. Religions affect a majority of the world's population and reach many different audiences across ethnic, national, economic, cultural, and political categories.

Adherents of a religion or a spiritual organization usually accept its ethical and moral teaching as well as the advice or guidance of its leadership. Many religions have significant economic resources and in some regions of the world are also politically influential. Even religions and spiritual traditions with comparatively small memberships and few economic resources have the ability to create social capital by building networks and strengthening social ties within communities. Although only recently recognizing environmental issues as a moral obligation based in sacred texts or teachings, many religions are now encouraging believers to respond to climate change issues. In the twenty-first century, religious leaders, religious institutions and organizations, and communities of religious or spiritual believers have been politically and socially involved in addressing climate change.

Although Hinduism's religious leaders were collaborating as early as the 1980s with the Alliance of Religions and Conservation (ARC) on environmental issues, it was not until the twenty-first century that they publicly released specific statements about climate change. In 2009 religious leaders submitted an initial Hindu Declaration on Climate Change at the Parliament of the World's Religions, followed by the 2015 Hindu Declaration on Climate Change submitted to the United Nations Framework Convention on Climate Change (UNFCCC). Citing numerous verses from Hinduism's sacred texts, the 2015 Hindu Declaration defines climate change as a problem for all of creation that must be addressed by governments and world leaders immediately.

Sharing some core beliefs with Hinduism such as karma, rebirth, and the interconnectedness of all life, Buddhist religious leaders have also supported the UNFCCC. Buddhist Thich Nhat Hanh, known for his global leadership and for developing engaged Buddhism, wrote *Falling in Love with the Earth* in 2014 in response to a request from the UNFCCC for a

Buddhist statement on climate change. The Dalai Lama also submitted a formal Buddhist statement for the 2015 Paris Agreement, defining climate change as a "problem which human beings created" that must be addressed by all people, including world leaders. Additional Buddhist religious leaders signed the Interfaith Climate Change Statement to World Leaders that was submitted to the UN in support of the Paris Agreement and have participated in the UN Faith for Earth Initiative launched in 2017 that addresses climate change and related UN Sustainable Development Goals (SDGs) set for 2030.

Throughout 2015 in support of the UNFCCC Paris Agreement, several leaders from Judaism, Christianity, and Islam joined Buddhism and Hinduism in advocating for governments to take action against climate change. These experienced leaders, who had been involved in religious environmentalism for years, asserted that political leaders and governments were morally obligated to ratify and sign the Paris Agreement. Rabbi Arthur Waskow, organizer of the progressive Shalom Center, had for more than forty years been integrating environmentalism into the major branches of Judaism, developing a distinctly Jewish environmentalism that has been influential in theology, activism, and daily worship. Pope Francis I, on behalf of the Catholic Church and Christianity, called for global "ecological conversion" in his 2015 encyclical *Laudato Si': On Care for Our Common Home*, with extensive attention given to environmental degradation caused by anthropogenic climate change. From Orthodox Christianity, Patriarch Bartholomew I proclaimed the sinfulness of ecologically destructive acts as early as the 1980s and has been an active supporter of the UNFCCC's 1997 Kyoto Protocol. Representing Islam, prominent imams, leaders, and scholars issued the 2015 Islamic Declaration on Global Climate Change, which urged all peoples and nations to act immediately and collaboratively to address the climate change crisis.

In addition to the statements from specific religions, 270 leaders from numerous religions collectively submitted the Interfaith Climate Change Statement to World Leaders in 2016 in support of the Paris Agreement. This interreligious statement noted the scientific evidence confirming anthropogenic climate change and urged that "we must begin a transition away from polluting fossil fuels and toward clean energy sources" and "strive for alternatives to the culture of consumerism that is so destructive to ourselves and to our planet."

In the twenty-first century, a majority of religious traditions have acknowledged anthropogenic climate change and are working to slow down its negative effects on human societies and the natural environment. Those branches of world religions with millions or even billions of adherents have significant political influence, seemingly unlimited material resources, and are likely to be invited to participate in national or international policy-making decisions related to climate change. Some smaller branches within the major world religions, even though they have fewer resources and less political influence, have also addressed anthropogenic climate change. For example, in 2006 the Evangelical Environmental Network (EEN) helped launch the Evangelical Climate Change Initiative, a campaign to raise climate change awareness that included publishing "A Call to Action" in the *New York Times*. Similarly, communities within Jainism and Sikhism have made formal statements on climate change and are encouraging lifestyles that can diminish anthropogenic climate change. Religious traditions outside of major world religions, such as Paganism, New Age spirituality, folk religions, nature religions, and others are also involved in fighting anthropogenic climate change but are not always included in interreligious dialogues and international politics.

See also: Alliance of Religions and Conservation; Bartholomew I of Constantinople; Buddhism; Christianity; Dalai Lama; Evangelical Environmental Network; Folk Religions; Hinduism; Judaism; *Laudato Si'*; Nature Religions; New Age Movement; Paris Agreement; Pope Francis I

Further Reading

Antal, Jim. 2018. *Climate Church, Climate World: How People of Faith Must Work for Change*. Lanham, MD: Rowman & Littlefield.

Chauhan, Pradeep S. 2019. *Climate Change and Paris Agreement: Challenges after US Withdrawal*. New Delhi: New Century Publications.

Intergovernmental Panel on Climate Change. 2015. *Climate Change 2014: Synthesis Report: Longer Report*. Geneva, Switzerland: Intergovernmental Panel on Climate Change.

Khalid, Fazlun M. 2019. *Signs on the Earth: Islam, Modernity and the Climate Crisis*. Markfield, UK: Kube Publishing.

Mason, Lisa Reyes, ed. 2019. *People and Climate Change: Vulnerability, Adaptation, and Social Justice*. New York: Oxford University Press.

D

Dalai Lama

The 14th Dalai Lama, Tenzin Gyatso, was born in 1935 to a rural agricultural family in northeastern Tibet. He assumed the spiritual title of Dalai Lama in 1939, and at age fifteen officially accepted all political, social, and spiritual duties of the position. In 1950 the People's Republic of China took control of Tibet, and after the 1959 Tibetan Uprising in Lhasa against Chinese occupational troops, the Dalai Lama and the Central Tibetan Administration were forced into permanent exile in Dharamsala, northern India. As Tibet's head of state in exile, Tenzin Gyatso was an international political advocate for the establishment of Tibet as a democratic and autonomous nation. As a globally recognized Buddhist spiritual leader, he has written and spoken extensively on nonviolence, environmentalism, economics, science, and the importance of interreligious dialogue. In 1989 he was awarded the Nobel Peace Prize for his commitment to finding a peaceful resolution for the conflict between Tibet and China and for his advocacy of nonviolence in general. In 2011 the Dalai Lama Tenzin Gyatso announced that although he would be continuing as the spiritual leader of Tibetan Buddhism, he was officially retired from his political position with the Central Tibetan Administration.

Tenzin Gyatso has advocated for a modern, balanced position clearly grounded in the teachings of the Buddha on important issues, such as abortion, sexuality, and the role of women. He has been more outspoken on some issues, such as nonviolence, animal welfare, and environmentalism, but he still clearly drew from Buddhist teachings. In his writings and comments, Tenzin Gyatso defines abortion as an act of killing that is, however, ethically permissible in some situations. On issues of sexuality, sexual orientation, and gender identity, he advocates the general Buddhist approach of "respect, tolerance, and the full recognition of human rights for all."

Similarly, he views women as equals and has commented that the next Dalai Lama might be female, although his related remarks in 2015 about the importance of a woman's physical attractiveness have drawn critique. Respect and kindness are common themes in his work, and Tenzin Gyatso has urged Tibetans and "all people to move toward a vegetarian diet that doesn't cause suffering" and to express compassion for all creatures. His advocacy work on environmental issues has included discussing water and land use, global warming and climate change, deforestation, and wildlife conservation.

The Dalai Lama has stated that if "there is one area in which both education and the media have a special responsibility, it is, I believe, our natural environment" and asserts that humans are the only species capable of both destroying the earth and protecting it. He has suggested many strategies over the years, such as reducing the use of wood and other natural resources, implementing family planning that lowers human impact on the natural environment, and designing factories that do not create pollution. Throughout his writings, Tenzin Gyatso has emphasized the importance of both individual and collective action. He has noted that "while one person's actions may not have a significant impact, the combined effect of millions of individuals' actions certainly does" and has been critical of the lifestyles of wealthy, developed nations. Similarly, he believes every individual should be involved, in whatever ways possible for each one, in protecting the natural environment of "Mother Earth" and all "her" living creatures. In his environmental advocacy that spans more than fifty years, Tenzin Gyatso has regularly discussed the importance of resource management, sustainability, the impact of human technology, and the problems associated with human population growth.

Tenzin Gyatso supported engaged Buddhism throughout his political and spiritual appointments as Dalai Lama, and provided inspiration, ideas, and spiritual leadership to both Buddhist and secular environmental activists around the world. In his 1987 five-point peace plan for Tibet, which led to his receiving the 1989 Nobel Peace Prize, he included the creation of laws that protect wildlife, all animals, and plant life; resource management that protects the ecosystem; and policies that support sustainable development. In the twenty-first century he has suggested these points as part of a model for global ecological awareness. Additionally, he has continued to teach that nonviolence and commitment to environmentalism are inseparable. Recently, these teachings were included in the 2019 launch of "Social, Emotional and Ethical Learning" (SEE Learning) in India, a new campaign to improve the educational and spiritual experiences of young people.

See also: Buddhism

Further Reading

Gyatso, Tenzin, and Sofia Stril-Rever. 2010. *My Spiritual Journey: Personal Reflections, Teachings, and Talks*. New York: HarperOne.

Daoism

Daoism, or Taoism, is a philosophical and religious tradition that originated in China more than 2,500 years ago. It was later formalized in the philosophical writings of Lao Tzu, dated at around the fourth century BCE. Inheriting elements of prehistoric Chinese folk religions and ancient Chinese philosophies, Daoism has continued to accumulate a variety of texts and practices that have provided the foundation for many different religious movements over the centuries. Although there are diverse interpretations and approaches in Daoism, all of them share a core belief in the Way (*dao*) of the Universe. The Way was not created by a deity or divine act but rather is seen as a constantly emerging creative process though which all things come into being or experience becoming their true selves. By the third century CE, during the Han dynasty, an organized Daoist tradition of religious orders, philosophers, hermits, and shamanic practitioners had formed in China's Sichuan region. Daoism has fallen in and out of favor politically over time, but currently it is one of several religious doctrines officially recognized in the People's Republic of China, with more than twenty million adherents mostly in China, Taiwan, Macau, and some areas of Southeast Asia.

Followers of Daoism seek to act in harmony with nature and believe the individual can achieve perfection by being in harmony with the flow of cosmic processes known as the *dao*. Although many Daoists believe human action goes against this cosmic flow, there is a great diversity of interpretation in contemporary Daoism regarding this point, with some arguing that activism can be part of human transformation and achievement of harmony. Some of the beliefs and practices of Daoism include following the Way (*dao*) to achieve immortality; individuals' need to find their own path in life within the natural world and through the Way or *dao* of the universe; balancing yin and yang to harmonize with nature; developing the chi (or ch'i or qi) of the body through meditation and disengagement; and recognizing the movement of matter and energy through the earth and its seasons. Because of this focus on harmony with the natural world, Daoist thought is often described as deeply ecological or environmentally friendly.

In the twenty-first century, many Daoists are finding ways to be involved in environmental activism without compromising their commitment to harmony and *wu-wei*, which is the spiritual tenet of accepting things as they are. In 2006 Daoist spiritual leaders in China wrote the Qinling Agreement, which pledged Daoist commitment to protecting the environment and created the Daoist Ecological Protection Network (DEPN). More than 120 Daoist temples implementing environmentally friendly practices, such as biofuel, solar power, and prevention of soil erosion, have joined DEPN, which is also supported by the Alliance of Religions and Conservation (ARC). Daoist monks, nuns, and others involved in DEPN emphasize protecting nature and pursuing environmental harmony, and they see their activism as nonintrusive, passive, organic, and in keeping with Daoist teachings.

See also: Alliance of Religions and Conservation; Folk Religions

Further Reading

Miller, James. 2017. *China's Green Religion: Daoism and the Quest for a Sustainable Future.* New York: Columbia University Press.

Deforestation

Deforestation refers to the intentional or unintentional process that occurs when forests are eradicated either through overharvesting or through converting the land for other purposes. Clear-cutting, burning, or gradual encroachment are all common methods of deforestation and are used by corporations, governments, independent farmers and ranchers, and Indigenous peoples. The causes and reasons for deforestation include urbanization, use of trees for fuel, logging operations, extraction of tree oils or other consumer products, conversion of forests into ranch or farmland, corporate agriculture, drilling or mining operations, and other human activities. As of 2019 approximately 30 percent of the planet's surface was covered by forests, with most scientific research predicting increases in deforestation that will negatively impact all life on Earth.

Deforestation affects the atmosphere, the hydrological cycle, soil, and biodiversity and is one of the primary factors contributing to global climate change. Forests absorb CO_2, which is the most harmful greenhouse gas and a primary cause of anthropogenic climate change. Increases in deforestation result in increases in CO_2 levels, which contribute to rising temperatures, rising sea levels, and extreme weather events. Forests are essential to the earth's hydrological cycle, capturing rain and snow, creating watersheds that drain into streams and rivers, and preventing soil erosion by slowing water runoff. Forests provide the root systems that anchor and protect soil from erosion by water and wind, and as deforestation increases, this anchoring system and the soil it protects are lost. Forests also provide habitat for more than 70 percent of the world's land-based plant and animal species, and deforestation results in loss of species and decreases in biodiversity.

In the twenty-first century, many scientists, politicians, research institutes, private foundations, and nongovernmental organizations have asserted that deforestation is a global crisis that must be addressed immediately. Religious and spiritual traditions, with their influence over billions of adherents, their extensive social relationships, and their economic investments have become increasingly important allies in combatting deforestation. In regions around the world, many communities have close ties to forests, sacred groves, and trees that are integral with their religious and spiritual traditions, with some also having traditional ecological knowledge (TEK) of local and regional forest ecosystems.

The Worldwatch Institute, an organization dedicated to accelerating the "transition to a sustainable world that meets human needs" and to addressing global environmental concerns, asserts that religions have assets that can help solve environmental problems such as deforestation. All types of religions, including world religions, Indigenous belief systems, and folk religions, have these assets, which include direct influence on people's worldviews, leaders with moral authority, many adherents, material resources, and the capacity to build communities and networks. Examples of religiously or spiritually motivated Indigenous activism that is focused on deforestation are found around the world in Africa, Asia, the Americas, and other regions. World religions, such as Buddhism,

Christianity, Hinduism, and Islam, are also involved in forest conservation both at the global level, through organizations such as the United Nations, and at the local level in communities dependent on the forest ecosystems.

Indigenous peoples around the world often have cosmologies and religious belief systems that include forest conservation practices, usually based on traditional ecological knowledge (TEK). The practices and beliefs of many of these Indigenous groups provide examples of resistance to deforestation, either through their recognized authority and participation in political decision-making, in their ability to resist encroachment by corporate developers, or by becoming environmental activists that challenge deforestation behaviors. The Ammatoan in Indonesia and the Grassy Narrows Ojibwe in Canada are two of the numerous examples of Indigenous groups that see themselves as spiritually inseparable from the forests in their ecosystems. Although the Ammatoan of Sulawesi, eastern Indonesia, converted to Islam in the seventeenth century, they have continued to practice their Indigenous religious traditions, which include the belief that the forests and humans have a reciprocal responsibility to care for each other. The Ammatoan's religious beliefs guide their interactions with the forest, which they divide into several categories or realms, with certain activities, such as felling trees, hunting, smoking out bees, or collecting firewood, either forbidden or allowed only in designated areas for specific reasons with the permission of community leaders. In Ontario, Canada, the Grassy Narrows Ojibwe believe that protecting their forests and ecosystems is an essential element of their spirituality, cultural identity, and ancestral continuity. The Grassy Narrows Ojibwe community has legally and politically opposed logging operations and the extraction of timber for paper on their lands, which they believe endanger their spiritual kin, comprising all species in the ecosystem.

In major world religions, religious leaders, theologians, and philosophers often develop theological or doctrinal positions on environmental issues, such as deforestation, based on interpretations of sacred texts. These theological and philosophical positions are then disseminated throughout the religion's networks, when imams, pastors, rabbis, lay instructors, and other religious authorities provide guidelines to their followers. For example, in Islam, the issue of deforestation is discussed in terms of forest conservation and is tied directly to the Qur'an and Hadith. Using these sacred texts, Islam's leading thinkers and religious leaders develop positions on forest conservation that are then taught to Muslims around the world, including guidelines for individual lifestyles, planning mosque activities, and implementing forest conservation in policy and law. The Qur'an provides the foundation for Muslims' beliefs about the natural world, with humans appointed by God as stewards (*khalifah*) of the earth. Humans, as God's representatives on earth, are instructed in the Qur'an to live in responsible and sustainable ways that protect creation for future generations. Because environmental stewardship is a religious obligation, the hima system, which regulates land usage, is also considered a religious obligation in Islam and commands that areas should be set aside for forest conservation. Additionally, Islam encourages planting trees as a type of charity for the betterment of humanity and all life, based on specific teachings in the Hadith. In the twenty-first century, Islam's religious leaders and academics have developed guidelines for forest conservation, disseminated the information globally to Muslims, and worked to integrate forest conservation into educational curricula and public policy, with organizations such as the Islamic Foundation for Ecology and Environmental Sciences (IFEES) representative of this trend.

As with Islam, other world religions have developed official positions on deforestation and forest conservation. In general, each religion's leading thinkers and scholars analyze environmental issues in the context of their sacred texts and practices, which then provides the foundation for an official statement on an issue. In the twenty-first century, leaders from world religions usually engage in collaboration with global organizations, such as the United Nations, and interreligious organizations, such as the Alliance of Religions and Conservation (ARC), that dedicate resources to forest conservation and reversing deforestation. For example, ARC, which operated from 1995 to 2019, worked with leaders from the world's major religions to promote forest conservation and reverse deforestation. ARC's forest conservation projects included working with the SANASI organization to map religious and sacred forests around the world, which in turn has helped religious organizations manage those forests.

ARC also worked with the Church of Sweden, to ensure that Sweden's forests are sustainably managed, and with Hindu groups that were establishing sustainable use practices in the sacred forests of Orissa, India. In 2011 Buddhist monks and nuns from Cambodia, Laos, Thailand, and Myanmar attended a conference sponsored by ARC that influenced Cambodian Buddhist monks to form Monks Community Forest (MCF) and the Independent Monk Network for Social Justice (IMNSJ). Both MCF and IMNSJ have been lobbying lawmakers and working with the government in Cambodia to prevent deforestation and to implement forest conservation policies. Although ARC officially ended as an organization in 2019, similar projects continue through global organizations such as the United Nations and numerous other affiliated religious and environmental organizations, with interreligious and international collaboration increasing on deforestation.

See also: Alliance of Religions and Conservation; Biodiversity; Climate Change; Folk Religions; Islamic Foundation for Ecology and Environmental Sciences; Nature Religions; Soil Conservation; Traditional Ecological Knowledge; Water

Further Reading

Catton, Theodore. 2016. *American Indians and National Forests.* Tucson: University of Arizona Press.

Forsyth, Tim, and Andrew Walker. 2008. *Forest Guardians, Forest Destroyers: The Politics of Environmental Knowledge in Northern Thailand.* Seattle: University of Washington Press.

Gardner, Gary T., and Worldwatch Institute. 2006. *Inspiring Progress: Religions' Contributions to Sustainable Development.* New York: W. W. Norton.

Horning, Nadia Rabesahala. 2018. *The Politics of Deforestation in Africa: Madagascar, Tanzania, and Uganda.* Cham, Switzerland: Palgrave Macmillan.

Maarif, Samsul. 2015. "Ammatoan Indigenous Religion and Forest Conservation." *Worldviews: Global Religions, Culture & Ecology* 19 (2): 144–60.

Runyan, Christiane, and Paolo D'Odorico. 2016. *Global Deforestation.* New York: Cambridge University Press.

E

Ecofeminism

Ecofeminism emerged in the 1970s as a political and social movement based in environmentalism and feminism, involving activists, academics, scientists, socialist ecofeminists, radical ecofeminists, cultural ecofeminists, religious or theological ecofeminists, and a range of followers of other approaches. Ecofeminists of all types assert that there is a historical connection between the exploitation of nature and the oppression of women and that both of these problems are the result of male domination in the economic, political, religious, and social spheres of society. Ecofeminists believe that society should be organized in an egalitarian way that eliminates both social inequality and the domination of other species by humans. In addition to eliminating patriarchy and social inequalities, the ecofeminist ideal includes creating sustainable societies that prioritize biodiversity and avoid destruction of the natural environment. Most ecofeminist thought and activism in the 1970s and 1980s originated in North America and Europe, but by the 1990s variations on ecofeminist thoughts could be found around the world from many different regions, cultures, and religious traditions.

Ecofeminist thought encompasses a wide range of thinkers, scholars, and activists, including feminists, political theorists, historians, practitioners of nature religions, ecotheologians, environmentalists, and others. Charlene Spretnak, a professor of religion and a leader in the ecofeminist and women's spirituality movements, has written extensively on nature-based religion and Goddess spirituality, as found in archeological records, historical sources, and contemporary ecofeminism. As a leading ecofeminist scholar and political leader, Spretnak has also examined the connection between feminism and women's careers in environmental studies, science, technology, and environmental policy, and how seminal ecofeminist thought was triggered by women's professional experiences in these fields.

Spretnak and other ecofeminists also note a conceptual, cultural, and symbolic connection between women and nature historically, for instance, in the depiction of men as dominant over women and nature in ancient Greco-Roman culture. According to many ecofeminists, this idea was perpetuated in Christianity and other religious institutions, and then finally incorporated into the scientific thought of modern Europe. Ecofeminist empirical research, which also focuses on the oppression of women and nature, has concluded that environmental problems and issues tend to affect women more than men globally, especially in regions where women must obtain food, water, and fuel for their family from the natural environment or local ecosystem. Contemporary ecofeminism argues that the domination of women and nature has been reinforced by religious, cultural, political, and economic institutions. These institutions, they argue, should be transformed into ecosocial institutions and societies that embrace spirituality, equality among all genders or sexes, and respect for the natural environment.

Ecofeminists in the 1970s had a critical interpretation of the Judeo-Christian tradition's role historically in the oppression of women and degradation of the natural environment. A majority of these ecofeminists were Christian scholars or scholars of religion who were trying both to understand the history of patriarchy in religious institutions and to integrate ecofeminist ideas into theology. Beginning in the 1970s, Rosemary Radford Ruether, a Christian theologian and prominent ecofeminist, asserted that women must challenge and transform society's "fundamental model of relationships" that is based on domination of one group by another. Only then, she notes, will women be liberated and able to help solve the ecological crisis and provide solutions for environmental issues and problems.

To begin this transformation of society, Ruether believes that women and their allies must merge the goals of both the environmental movement and the women's movement. They will then be able to begin a "radical reshaping" of societal values and economic, social, and political relations, which will then provide the foundation for egalitarian and environmentally sustainable societies. She explains in her biblically based vision of social justice that humans "need an entirely new way of organizing human production and consumption in relation to natural resources, one that both distributes the means of life more justly among all earth's people and also uses resources in a way that renews them from generation to generation." Ruether is representative of many Christian ecofeminists, who usually encourage interreligious and intercultural cooperation on environmental issues.

Hindu activist, scholar, and scientist Vandana Shiva began writing from an ecofeminist perspective in the 1980s. All of her activism, research, and writing has since been grounded in ecofeminist principles that emphasize the importance of women's labor and spirituality in India and around the world. She also frames her writing and activism as a radical critique of masculine dominance, colonialism, and globalization. Shiva, like most ecofeminists, is opposed to war and capitalism because they are seen as patriarchal structures that perpetuate a culture of male domination, exploitation of the natural world, and social inequality. In her writing and presentations, Shiva asserts that women can only achieve true liberation by protecting all life on the planet and working to abolish patriarchy and capitalism locally, regionally, and globally. Shiva argues that capitalism, corporate globalization, and colonialism are directly connected to oppression and violence against women, and her work has focused mostly on the consequences for women in lower income, rural, or less economically developed regions of the world. Shiva refers to her approach as political or "subsistence" ecofeminism, and much of her research and activism is directly involved with women and subsistence agriculture. As with most ecofeminists, Shiva also emphasizes the importance of women's spirituality and their symbolic relationship with nature.

Ecofeminist thinking is also found in Buddhism, but there is more evidence for its presence in North America than in Asia and other regions. In 2017 Emma Tomalin began documenting contemporary ecofeminist Buddhist thought, including possible ecofeminist Buddhist writers and case studies of contemporary communities. Tomalin identifies threads of a Buddhist ecofeminism in the work of a few Buddhist scholars and communities, including the writing of Theravada practitioner Thanissara and the activist Buddhist nunnery Aloka Vihara, located in California. The Buddhists in these two examples are committed to replacing male domination in Buddhism with social equality, working for full ordination for women in Buddhism, and practicing engaged Buddhism through environmental activism.

Tomalin also identifies examples of ecofeminist thought in Buddhist nuns in Asia involved in environmental activism, such as the work of the Buddhist nun Jiyul Sunim. Scholar Eun-Su Cho has asserted that Jiyul Sunim, who protested construction in South Korea that would destroy the habitat of several species, has developed a distinctly Korean Buddhist ecofeminism. These and the additional examples of Buddhist ecofeminism identified by Tomalin share the assumptions that Buddhism historically has been a patriarchal religion that contributed to the exploitation and oppression of both women and Earth's natural environment. When compared to the Judeo-Christian tradition, however, Buddhism has relatively few writers and leaders who identify as ecofeminist.

Ecofeminists are also active in alternative spiritualities and new religious movements, with these types of theorists, thinkers, and activists usually referred to as cultural ecofeminists. Cultural ecofeminists often create distinct feminist spiritualities that celebrate women and nature, and intentionally avoid practices and beliefs found in patriarchal religious traditions. Nature religions, Goddess or Gaia worship, Paganism, Indigenous belief systems, and New Age beliefs are common sources of cultural ecofeminist spiritualities. In regions of the world where women have achieved high levels of social, political, and economic equality and there is support for environmentally friendly lifestyles, cultural ecofeminism is found in a variety of alternative spiritualities and new religious movements. Several prominent cultural ecofeminists in economically developed, globalized, and postindustrial regions of the world are adherents of nature religions or Paganism. However, in many other regions globally, women still struggle daily with securing food and shelter and do not have access to education or political power. In these regions, ecofeminism is more likely to be gradually introduced into existing religious traditions as well as being extremely important in the pursuit of basic social equality and in replacing ideologies that dominate or oppress women and the natural world.

See also: Ecotheology; Gaia Hypothesis; Nature Religions; New Age Movement; Shiva, Vandana

Further Reading

Ruether, Rosemary Radford. 2005. *Integrating Ecofeminism, Globalization, and World Religions*. Lanham, MD: Rowman & Littlefield.

Shiva, Vandana, Ariel Salleh, and Maria Mies. 2014. *Ecofeminism*. London: Zed Books.

Spretnak, Charlene. 1982. *The Politics of Women's Spirituality: Essays on the Rise of Spiritual Power within the Feminist Movement*. Garden City, NY: Anchor Books.

Tomalin, Emma. 2017. "Gender and the Greening of Buddhism: Exploring Scope for a Buddhist Ecofeminism in an Ultramodern Age." *Journal for the Study of Religion, Nature and Culture* 11 (4): 455–80.

Ecotheology

Ecotheology is a theological approach that combines the fields of theology and ecology. Theology is the study of the nature of God, gods, and the divine, and ecology is a scientific field that studies organisms or creatures and their habitats and ecosystems. Ecotheology is critical of contemporary society and argues that humans should take care of the earth in a way that is both sustainable and grounded in religious traditions and sacred texts or practices. Ecotheologians are found in diverse religious traditions and usually are involved in practicing religiously motivated environmentalism in their communities, as well as being scholars and academics. Ecotheology attempts to transform traditional religion by discovering, examining, and reinterpreting sacred texts and religious practices in the context of environmentalism.

Ecotheology emerged as a branch of theology by the late 1960s in response to some scholars, scientists, and activists claiming that the Judeo-Christian tradition had been involved in spreading religious ideas that encouraged the exploitation and destruction of the natural environment. There were a few Christian theologians prior to the 1960s, such as Pierre Teilhard de Chardin, as well as thinkers in many other religious traditions that explored the relationship between humans, other creatures, and the natural environment. In the 1970s feminist scholar and Catholic theologian Rosemary Radford Ruether integrated ecofeminism with ecotheology, asserting along with many ecotheologians that human domination of all creatures had wrongly been historically justified using Judeo-Christian texts. Although ecotheological works were initially found mostly in the Christian and Jewish traditions, by the 1970s there were ecotheologians in several religious traditions, such as Vandana Shiva in Hindu ecotheology, Seyyid Hossein Nasr's Islamic ecotheology, and the Buddhist-influenced environmentalism of Fritz Schumacher. Additionally, Christian theologian Thomas Berry, influenced by Teilhard de Chardin and James Lovelock's Gaia Hypothesis, represents a trend in some ecotheological scholarship beginning in the 1970s that is heavily and overtly reliant on scientific research.

In the twenty-first century, ecotheology has become a distinct academic field and an essential element of religious environmentalism. Rabbi Lawrence Troster, a leading Jewish ecotheologian and religious environmentalist, has identified several characteristics of contemporary ecotheology. Troster traces the foundations of ecotheology to modern science, with its research and many discoveries giving support to the main premise of ecotheology: that all creatures and natural phenomenon are interdependent, divinely created elements of a planetary ecosystem. Additionally, Troster notes that many ecotheologians reference personal stories that emphasize a sense of place or attachment to the surrounding natural environment, including animal, plants, landscapes, waterscapes, and climates. Troster and other ecotheologians have also found that ecofeminism, with its criticism of male domination, continues to have a very strong influence on contemporary ecotheology.

See also: Ecofeminism; Gaia Hypothesis; Teilhard de Chardin, Pierre; White, Lynn Townsend, Jr.

Further Reading

Dalton, Anne Marie, and Henry C. Simmons. 2010. *Ecotheology and the Practice of Hope.* SUNY Series on Religion and the Environment. Albany: State University of New York Press.

Troster, Lawrence. 2013. "What Is Eco-Theology?" *CrossCurrents* 63 (4): 380–85.

Energy

Energy sources generate electricity, combustion, and other types of power for a wide range of human endeavors, such as communication, refrigeration, heating, lighting, transportation, computing, agriculture, and innumerable other activities. Energy sources can be either renewable or nonrenewable, and either primary, such as burning wood to create heat, or secondary, such as converting solar energy into electricity used in a home. Petroleum products, natural gas, hydrocarbon gas liquids, coal, and nuclear energy are all nonrenewable energy sources that cannot be replenished within a human lifetime or even within several generations. Solar energy, biomass from plants, geothermal energy, hydropower, and wind energy are all renewable energy sources that do not completely deplete or can be replenished within a human lifetime. The United Nations has defined "affordable and clean energy" as a sustainable development goal (SDG) to be achieved globally by 2030. The UN 2030 SDG for energy includes the following: affordable, reliable energy services; increased use of renewable energy; double the global rate of energy efficiency; enhanced international cooperation on clean energy; and expanded infrastructure and upgrade technology for sustainable energy services in developing countries. In addition to energy goals shared by the world's nations, the environmental risks associated with offshore drilling, nuclear power, hydraulic fracturing, coal mining, and other nonrenewable energy sources are a source of urgent concern for governments, activists, and the general public.

Religious environmental organizations focusing on energy issues are primarily concerned about anthropogenic climate change and its causes, such as pollution and emissions created by unrenewable energy sources. These organizations, whether specifically dedicated to energy issues or to environmental sustainability in general, are involved in the promotion of energy conservation, protecting the health of ecosystems and the public, and campaigning for sustainable and clean energy policies. Nonrenewable energy is seen by these organizations as contributing to environmental problems, such as climate change, pollution, soil infertility and erosion, destruction of ecosystems, and loss of biodiversity.

Religious environmental organizations use diverse approaches and strategies in their projects and initiatives addressing energy and related issues.

Some religious organizations actively campaign for regional, national, and international policies that support transitioning from unrenewable to renewable energy sources. Other organizations work to change the lifestyles of religious adherents in local communities, focus on corporate and economic sector accountability, or sponsor research and workshops on energy issues. Interfaith Power and Light (IPL), the National Religious Partnership for the Environment (NRPE), the Islamic Foundation for Ecology and Environmental Sciences (IFEES), the Alliance of Religions and Conservation (ARC), and the Evangelical Environmental Network (EEN) are just a few of the many religious organizations working on energy-related issues. Additionally, there are numerous Indigenous organizations rooted in traditional spirituality that are attempting to prevent extraction of nonrenewable energy sources from their homelands.

Globally there are religious organizations directly involved with the energy issues specific to their country or region. In the United States there are several organizations and communities that have actively campaigned against unrenewable energy sources. The National Religious Partnership on the Environment (NRPE), a U.S. interreligious collaboration among the United States Conference of Catholic Bishops, the National Council of Churches, the Coalition of Jewish Communities and Environment, and the

EEN, opposes oil and gas drilling in public waters and on public lands. NRPE has continuously pressured U.S. Congress to oppose offshore drilling and other petroleum and gas extraction techniques.

Interfaith Power and Light (IPL), another U.S. interreligious environmental organization, campaigns for renewable energy and in 2017 publicly opposed U.S. president Trump's Executive Order 13783 on Promoting Energy Independence and Economic Growth. In 2019 IPL objected to the appointment of former coal lobbyist Andrew Wheeler as U.S. Environmental Protection Agency (EPA) Administrator, asserting that because of Wheeler's association with the coal industry, he would likely reverse or eliminate existing EPA clean energy policies.

Several Indigenous communities in the United States also actively oppose nonrenewable energy and extraction industries that destroy their sacred lands. The Lumbee Indians, the Texas Society of Native Nations, and the Standing Rock Sioux are just a few examples of communities that actively protest and campaign against pipelines, hydraulic fracturing, and other techniques used in methane gas and petroleum operations in the United States.

See also: Alliance of Religions and Conservation; Evangelical Environmental Network; Hydraulic Fracturing; Interfaith Power and Light; Islamic Foundation for Ecology and Environmental Sciences; Marine Conservation; National Religious Partnership for the Environment; Overpopulation; Paris Agreement; Sustainability

Further Reading

Koehrsen, Jens. 2015. "Does Religion Promote Environmental Sustainability? Exploring the Role of Religion in Local Energy Transitions." *Social Compass* 62 (3): 296–310.

Usher, Bruce. 2019. *Renewable Energy: A Primer for the Twenty-First Century.* Columbia University Earth Institute Sustainability Primers. New York: Columbia University Press.

Environmental Justice

Environmental justice is a term used to describe the fair and equal treatment of all people regarding environmental laws and policies, regardless of ethnicity, race, income level, or any other characteristics. The concept emerged in the late 1960s in the United States, when citizens and activists noted that some communities or categories of people were more likely to be subjected to environmental risks, such as low-income neighborhoods being exposed to industrial toxins or ethnic minorities being excluded from important decisions related to environmental policy. By the 1980s a grassroots social movement had emerged in the United States that focused on environmental justice as a civil rights issue. Academics and scholars in the United States brought further attention to environmental justice during the 1990s in numerous studies and research projects. By the twenty-first century, an international environmental justice movement had developed drawing from decades of experiences worldwide and focusing on equal protection for all people regarding environmental risks, including health hazards, pollution and waste, corporate industrial dumping, and equal access to related decision-making processes. Because of their close connections to the local and regional communities they serve, as well as being motivated by their values and beliefs, many religious leaders have been continuously involved in environmental justice activism.

The concept of environmental justice provides a framework for assisting communities that experience increased risks from environmental hazards because of a community's characteristics, such as geographic location, education level, ethnicity, race, income level, or any other communal attributes. Environmental justice can be applied to cases within national, state, or regional boundaries, and it can also be applied to international global cases, such as a high-income country or a multinational corporation exporting toxic waste to low-income regions of the world. Using an environmental justice model, the stakeholders, conflicts, claims, problems, and issues of each case are identified. For example, in a case involving air quality, stakeholders might be a particular neighborhood, a nearby manufacturing plant, a public health clinic, and the American Lung Association. There might be competing claims, such as the manufacturing plant representatives asserting that they are *not* the cause of increased respiratory disease in the community and the public health clinic asserting that the manufacturing plant *is* the cause. There will likely be several additional issues, such as the community's poverty level, the community's access to decision-making in local government, and any other issue related to the location and operation of a manufacturing plant so close to a residential community. Whether a situation is local, regional, or international, if it involves the environment and is identified as possibly violating human rights or civil rights, then it is a matter of environmental justice.

The Christian approach to environmental justice is based in the belief that all community members should have equal access to the resources and decision-making process in their community. Christians also ground their environmental justice practices in biblical texts that emphasize the moral importance of attending to the needs of the "least among us," such as those who are marginalized, poor, oppressed, or disadvantaged. The United Farm Workers (UFW) union is an early example of Christian environmental justice efforts in the United States. The founders of UFW, organizers Cesar Chavez and Dolores Huerta, drew inspiration from Catholic social teaching and incorporated Catholic masses, symbols, and biblical texts into UFW organizing efforts to ban DDT and other harmful pesticides. UFW leaders publicized environmentally induced risks, such as the high rates of birth defects and cancer among low-income, minority farm workers, as moral issues that must be addressed by the United States and by consumers in general.

Similarly, the United Church of Christ (UCC) explicitly framed toxic dumping in rural North Carolina black-majority communities as an environmental justice issue in the 1980s. UCC church leaders organized congregations and staged public protests that used religious symbols, songs, prayers, and other texts to present environmental justice as Christian activism. UCC was instrumental in publicizing environmental justice in the United States, and its 1987 UCC *Toxic Wastes and Race Report* concluded that hazardous waste sites were much more likely to be located in areas where racial minorities lived.

Adherents of Hinduism have incorporated explicitly environmental justice approaches into environmental activism for several decades, such as is in the Chipko Movement. In the 1970s, subsistence farmers and villagers formed the Chipko Movement to protect trees and ecosystems in the Indian Himalayas. Members of the Chipko Movement incorporated Hindu symbols and Gandhian concepts, such as the *satyagraha* tradition of nonviolent protest, into their protests against loggers and manufacturers. Vandana Shiva, ecofeminist scholar and activist, documented the Chipko Movement as an example of environmental justice that involves primarily rural women involved in subsistence agriculture and viewed by corporate developers and logging companies as insignificant or powerless.

For Shiva and other Indian and Hindu scholars, the Chipko activists clearly framed their struggle as one of environmental justice, in which marginalized communities dependent on their ecosystems were more likely to be the victims of environmentally destructive corporate development. The Chipko activists were also clearly motivated, empowered, and driven by Hindu religious traditions, and they recited Hindu religious texts and performed Hindu religious rituals during protests and other actions. The influence of the Chipko Movement in India and surrounding regions continues as activists motivated by Hindu religious traditions and the concept of environmental justice protect forests and the ecosystems of rural villages against destructive corporate practices.

Currently there are several Muslim organizations that focus on environmental justice, primarily in the United States and the UK. Ecologist Huda Alkaff, one of the recognized White House Champions for Change in 2015, is the founder of Wisconsin Green Muslims, an environmental justice organization launched in 2005. In 2018 Alkaff explained the environmental justice principles followed by Wisconsin Green Muslims: "To ensure public involvement of low-income and minority groups in decision-making, preventing disproportionately high adverse impacts of decisions on low-income and minority groups, and ensuring low-income and minority groups receive a proportionate share of benefits." Wisconsin Green Muslims exemplify how numerous activists and organizations become involved in environmental justice because of their religious tradition or spiritual path. When designing and implementing their projects, such as the Faith and Solar Initiative and the Faithful Rainwater Harvesting Project, Wisconsin Green Muslims strive for "inclusion and equity for marginalized communities" and work with various mosques, other religions, and secular environmental groups. As Muslims, their approach is based in the Qur'an and their faith tradition of Islam, both of which provide the values and motivation for providing social, educational, financial, and spiritual opportunities for the communities they work with.

In the twenty-first century, there has been an increase in international organizations and global networks dedicated to environmental justice. Although organizations around the world are different in their circumstances and characteristics, they experience similar challenges in their efforts to empower disadvantaged communities. The Global Alliance for Incinerator Alternatives (GAIA) is an example of an international environmental justice network. Originally headquartered in the Philippines with members from more than ninety countries, GAIA coordinates members' efforts to reduce waste streams, eliminate hazardous incineration of waste, fight disposable plastics pollution, and support recycling and waste pickers' rights. GAIA focuses on representing disadvantaged communities, in countries around the world and with diverse religious and cultural backgrounds, that are threatened by environmental hazards and risks. As an alliance based on principles of environmental justice, GAIA helps these communities find common ground and achieve their shared goals through community-based solutions, changes in government and corporate policies and practices, and networks built across political and social boundaries. GAIA is representative of the increasingly international cooperation among activists and organizations focused on environmental justice issues, building interreligious and intercultural networks, and the sharing of knowledge.

See also: Ecofeminism; Ecotheology; Shiva, Vandana

Further Reading

Bauman, Whitney A., Richard Bohannon, and Kevin J. O'Brien, eds. 2010. *Grounding Religion: A Field Guide to the Study of Religion and Ecology*. Florence: Routledge.

Gade, Anna M. 2019. *Muslim Environmentalisms: Religious and Social Foundations*. New York: Columbia University Press.

Shiva, Vandana. 2015. *Soil Not Oil: Environmental Justice in an Age of Climate Crisis*. Berkeley, CA: North Atlantic Books.

Watt, Alan J. 2010. *Farm Workers and the Churches: The Movement in California and Texas*. College Station: Texas A&M University Press.

Evangelical Environmental Network

The Evangelical Environmental Network (EEN) is a U.S.-based Christian organization founded in 1993 that advocates for political action and public policies that "honor God and protect the environment." EEN consists of individuals, congregations, and several religious and secular organizations as well as other national and international environmental networks. EEN creates educational material for individuals, school groups, and congregations and provides opportunities for environmentally related service work.

It is also a politically engaged organization that influences politics and public policy on environmental issues by grassroots organizing and extensive use of digital social media. EEN developed a "Caring for Creation Pledge" that outlines Christian environmental stewardship for members and publishes educational material on evangelical Christian environmentalism for different age groups. Additionally, EEN is involved in disseminating information on elected officials and holding accountable those politicians and administrations that fail to support EEN's concept of a biblically mandated stewardship of the earth.

In 1995, EEN organized evangelical Christians to save the U.S. Endangered Species Act (ESA), which EEN asserted was being weakened by the U.S. Congress and special interest groups. EEN asserted that the ESA was a contemporary version of the biblical Noah's Ark. This comparison increased support for the ESA from conservative politicians, who were concerned that a large religious constituency saw ESA as biblically mandated Christian stewardship. In the mid-1990s, EEN worked with the Coalition of Christian Colleges and Universities, evangelical seminaries, and evangelical student groups to begin "earth-care training" in religious higher-education institutions. By the early 2000s EEN had started several "Creation Care" stewardship programs that were adopted across the United States, including the "What Would Jesus Drive?" campaign against SUVs and carbon emissions in general. In 2006 EEN helped launch the Evangelical Climate Change Initiative, a campaign to raise climate change awareness that included publishing "A Call to Action" in the *New York Times*.

EEN's current campaigns educate and politically mobilize evangelical Christians in response to several issues, including methane pollution, pro-life clean energy, water pollution, mercury and the unborn, microplastics pollution, and protection of U.S. public lands. EEN's educational efforts include writing and distributing materials, such as the children's book *Terry the Sea Turtle and the Terrible Plastic Straw*, educational materials for young adults, and eco-evangelical-themed blogs for parents. Since the early 2000s EEN has been regularly funded by politically progressive donors such as the Rockefeller Brothers Fund, Pew Charitable Trusts, and the William and Flora Hewett Foundation. Although its members are typically political conservatives, EEN has encountered opposition from some conservative Christians, including those who support the U.S. coal industry, reject EEN's position on CO_2 reductions, or reject the scientific claim that humans cause significant climate change. Since its inception, EEN has conducted several successful campaigns to influence political decisions and corporate behavior as well as national and international environmental policies and practices.

See also: Christianity; Climate Change; Pollution

Further Reading

Hescox, Mitch, and Paul Douglas. 2016. *Caring for Creation: The Evangelical's Guide to Climate Change and a Healthy Environment*. Minneapolis, MN: Bethany House.

F

Folk Religions

The term *folk religions* refers to attitudes, beliefs, and practices that are based in regional ethnic culture and are relatively unorganized when compared to formal or official religious institutions and doctrine. Folk religions, including popular belief, vernacular religion, and folk culture in general, are found in major religions, such as Islam, Christianity, Hinduism, as well as being a collection of regional subcultures, such as in Chinese folk religion. Folk religion has been studied increasingly since the 1960s, although there has not always been agreement among scholars about the definition and utility of the term itself. In the past, a few scholars asserted that the term *folk religion* had been used to reinforce economic and social class differences among different groups or cultures. However, most twenty-first century scholars who study folk religion use the term in their research and writing to emphasize the regional, ethnic, or subcultural aspect of religious or spiritual practices. Folk religion can refer to the religious aspect of local culture or the syncretism between a formal religion and popular folk practices.

In the latter half of the twentieth century, anthropologists and others who studied culture and religion offered several definitions of folk religion. In the 1970s, Don Yoder, a U.S. professor of religious studies and folklore, offered a delineated description of folk religion that has continued to influence research on folk religion around the world into the twenty-first century. Yoder suggested that there were at least five distinct ways of defining folk religion and that it was different in organization and structure from institutional religion. First, noted Yoder, folk religion represents the remnants of "beliefs and behavior inherited from earlier stages of the culture's development," such as the presence of pre-Christian beliefs and practices in European Catholic communities. Second, folk religion could be the mixture of an "official" religion with an ethnic religion, such as the syncretic belief systems resulting from the blending of Indigenous beliefs with Christianity or Islam.

Yoder's third perspective is reflective of somewhat outdated folkloric studies and defines certain folk religion practices as "fringe phenomena" and superstition or "the interaction of belief, ritual, custom, and mythology in traditional societies." Yoder identifies a fourth possible definition of folk religion as "the deposit in culture of folk religiosity, the full range of folk attitudes to religion" exemplified by "local folk arts, religious folk music, festivals, calendar customs, and other similar creations." Combining the other four definitions, Yoder offered a fifth definition as a "practical working definition" that defines folk religion as "the totality of all those views and practices of religion that exist among the people apart from and alongside the strictly theological and liturgical forms of the official religion."

Recent quantitative studies on folk religion use definitions that are similar to Yoder's. The Pew Research Center defines folk religions as "closely tied to a particular people, ethnicity or tribe" with some folk religions described as blending world religions with local customs and beliefs, as well as some not having sacred texts or formal doctrines. The Pew Center cites African traditional religions, Australian aboriginal religions, Chinese folk religions, and Native American religions as examples of folk religions. Using this definition, the Pew Research Center estimated that as of 2010, there were around 405 million adherents of folk or traditional religions globally, with a projected increase to 450 million by 2050.

Since some regions of the world stigmatize participation in religious or spiritual subcultures that are outside of formal or official religious institutions, it is likely that many individuals would not openly identify with folk religion subcultures. Considering the different elements of the definition of folk religion, the Pew Center's 2010 figures are possibly an underestimation of the number of people participating in these types of religious traditions. Although statistics such as those published by the Pew Center provide a general figure of the number of adherents, the presence of environmentalist behaviors in folk religion communities is best understood by examining recent studies of their experiences.

Ming-Sho Ho's 2005 study of an antipollution protest focuses on how folk religion provided the means for mobilizing collective action around environmental issues in a traditional village in Taiwan. In 1987 villagers from the Houchin community near Kaohsiung City collectively opposed an expansion project of the state-owned China Petroleum Company. This organized opposition marked the emergence of the Houchin antipollution movement that lasted three years. In 1990 the Houchin movement ran out of resources and was unable to continue resisting state-sponsored police repression, and the government then proceeded to build a naphtha-cracking facility and open it for production by 1994. By interviewing participants in the Houchin movement, Ho identified folk religion as essential to the shared motivations, beliefs, and collective identity that sustained the movement through its three years of continuous conflict and protest. Ho defines folk religion as the "ensemble of ritual and faith as practiced in a geographical unit" and in this case found that Houchin community members shared the "same religion by worshipping the patron god, managing the community temple, and financing festival activities" in their village. The Houchin community's localized folk religion provided a preexisting collective identity, language from religious ceremonies that was used in protest events, and the basis for the solidarity of the villagers as they went up against the much stronger state-sponsored China Petroleum Company.

Contemporary ecovillages in Hungary provide another example of the influence of folk religion on environmental activism and environmentally friendly lifestyles. In her 2018 study, Judit Farkas examined how Hungarian ecovillagers have constructed their own belief system from elements of folk religion or *native faith*, which is a term used by many Eastern European scholars and practitioners of nature religion or Paganism. Similarly, the Research Group of Modern Mythologies, a Hungarian organization that focuses on Neo-paganism, uses the term *ethnopaganism* when referring to folk religion. Hungarian ecovillagers themselves most frequently refer to their belief system as both nature faith and ecospirituality, explaining that it informs the design of their ecovillages, which include chemical-free farming, renewable energy, reduced consumption, recycling, and sustainable waste management.

Gabor Geczy, a physicist, a popular writer in the Hungarian native faith communities, and a prominent leader in the Hungarian ecovillage movement, asserts that Hungarians are obligated to heal the earth. Geczy teaches that Hungarians have been divinely protected by the Carpathian Basin's geography and that this protection ensured the survival of Hungarians so that they could ultimately heal the world. In her study on Hungarian ecovillages, which includes interviews with ecovillagers and their references to native faith leaders such as Geczy, Farkas concludes that the Hungarian native faith tradition, or folk religion, has been essential to the conceptualization, development, and social life of Hungarian ecovillages and their environmentally friendly practices and activism.

Eliza Kent's 2013 study on folk Hinduism is another example of recent research on the relationship between folk religion and environmentalism. Using interviews with villagers, Forest officers, historical and official state documents, Hindu sacred texts, and other sources, Kent examines the folk religion of Tamil villagers in the southern Indian state of Tamil Nadu. She documents how the beliefs, behaviors, and practices of their folk Hinduism support the protection of sacred trees, groves, and forests around the villages and wild areas of this region. In the Tamil Nadu region, there are oral traditions that go back thousands of years and that associate trees with sacred places and deities. There are local and regional beliefs—not necessarily mentioned in Hindu sacred texts—that assume gods and goddesses are present or inhabit the groves and forests, that the trees belong to the deity of a specific place, and that cutting the trees is forbidden because they belong to the deity. Regional oral folk traditions include stories about individuals and communities receiving divine punishment for cutting trees, and these stories act as a further protection of sacred groves. Folk religion practices include sustainable use of trees, groves, and forests, with fruits collected from sacred trees providing feasts at annual festivals held in honor of each god or goddess of a specific grove.

Although not all folk religions involve environmentalism, they often include traditional ecological knowledge (TEK) that encourages sustainability and environmentally friendly lifestyles. Scholars, activists, and adherents of folk religion continue to use the term to describe belief systems that protect local and regional ecosystems and shape the collective identity that reinforces a community's commitment to protecting its ecosystem. Folk religions, including Indigenous spiritual traditions, ethnopaganism, and a range of other regionally or ethnically grounded belief systems, often involve a deep love of the landscape or homeland and a commitment to protection of the natural environment. In the twenty-first century, scholars and researchers are showing an increased interest in understanding the connection between folk religion and environmentalism. Interviews that document the lived experience of folk religion adherents, historical studies that highlight the role of nature in folk practices and folk religions, and quantitative studies that measure attitudes toward the natural environment among adherents of folk religions are just a few of the approaches currently pursued by scholars.

See also: Animism; Nature Religions; Paganism; Traditional Ecological Knowledge

Further Reading

Farkas, Judit. 2018. "Nature Faith and Native Faith as Integrative Spiritualities in Hungarian Ecovillages." *Journal for the Study of Religion, Nature & Culture* 12 (2): 125–46.

Ho, Ming-Sho. 2005. "Protest as Community Revival: Folk Religion in a Taiwanese Anti-Pollution Movement." *African & Asian Studies* 4 (3): 237–69.

Kent, Eliza F. 2013. *Sacred Groves and Local Gods: Religion and Environmentalism in South India.* Oxford: Oxford University Press.

Pew Research Center. 2015. *The Future of World Religions: Population Growth Projections, 2010–2050.* Washington, DC: Pew Research Center.

Yoder, Don. 1974. "Toward a Definition of Folk Religion." *Western Folklore* 33 (1): 2–15.

Food Security

The term *food security* refers to the ideal food situation for human populations, including food availability, food access, food utilization, and food stability. As a concept, food security emerged in the 1970s through international discussions of global food supplies, food prices, and food availability, within the context of environmental issues such as climate change, increased human population, social and political conflicts, and numerous environmental stressors. Initially, in collaborations such as the World Food Conference of 1974, the issues of concern were famine, hunger, and food supply, with human behavior, demand, and access added to formal definitions of food security by the 1990s. As defined by the Food and Agriculture Organization (FAO) of the United Nations at the 1996 World Food Summit, food security exists "when all people, at all times, have physical and economic access to sufficient, safe and nutritious food to meet their dietary needs and food preferences for an active and healthy life." Currently, there are numerous global organizations that focus on availability of nutritious food, access to sufficient quantities of food, and consumption of properly stored and safe food for all individuals and for all members of households. Additionally, these organizations often track regional, national, and global food supply chains to ensure and manage stability of food supplies.

Although interreligious conflicts that jeopardize food security have increased globally in the twenty-first century, religions are also uniquely positioned to assist governments, nongovernmental organizations, and the private economic sector in their efforts to address food security issues. Religious teachings related to food security are usually focused on sustainable agricultural practices and alleviating hunger. The Abrahamic traditions of Judaism, Christianity, and Islam all emphasize the moral obligation to feed the hungry and share food with those in need. Additionally, Judaism and Islam have the *shmita* year and *hima* system, respectively, both of which involve land use practices that are related to food security. Judaism's *shmita* year, defined in the Torah's Book of Exodus as an agricultural practice required of Israel, includes instructions to let the land rest and redistribute food reserves to the needy every seventh year. Islam's *hima* system regulates land usage and defines sustainable agriculture and environmental conservation as religious obligations.

Although both the *shmita* year and *hima* system originally focused on agricultural practices, Judaism and Islam are now global religions that increasingly focus on humanitarian aspects of these practices, such as food security for all. Contemporary Hinduism and Buddhism also teach that food security is a moral or ethical obligation rooted in sacred texts, with Buddhism defining food security as compassion and loving-kindness, and Hinduism referencing *annadānam*, or the sacred duty to share food. Other religions also have food-sharing practices based in sacred text or tradition, such as Sikhism's global practice of *langar*, or community kitchen, which offers free vegetarian meals to all visitors.

Some religiously motivated organizations focus on food security within their own religious tradition, while others approach food security as a global issue requiring universal outreach. Buddhist Global Relief (BGR), Muslim Hands, and Bread for the World are a few of the many religious organizations dedicated to addressing food security globally for all people. BGR sponsors long-term projects related to food security rather than emergency relief, is staffed primarily by Buddhists, serves people of all backgrounds and religions, and is committed to interreligious collaborations. BGR's emphasis is on permanent, sustainable food production and distribution in the world's poorest communities, and on teaching sustainable farming techniques such as seed banking, rainwater harvesting, soil conservation, composting, and planting cash crops in community gardens. BGR also sponsors projects that teach women entrepreneurial skills and provide training in schools to improve children's nutrition.

Similarly, Muslim Hands (MH) serves impoverished communities around the world but also provides emergency food aid in addition to helping communities become environmentally sustainable. Although MH serves people of all backgrounds and religions, its staff and volunteers are primarily Muslim. MH focuses primarily on the alleviation of hunger and the implementation of projects that contribute to food security, such as planting orchards rather than clear-cutting land. Using different strategies from BGR and MH, Bread for the World (BW) is a Christian organization that works to eliminate hunger and is representative of organizations that address food security by focusing on legislation and policy making. BW's advocacy is focused almost exclusively on writing letters to U.S. politicians and leaders, urging them to support legislation that addresses hunger in the United States and around the world. BW's 2019 Offering of Letters campaign urged the U.S. government to end hunger by 2030 by increasing funding for global nutrition programs. Religious organizations that address food security are very diverse in their organizational structure and strategies. BGR and MH provide examples of organizations that address hunger and sponsor food security projects around the world, and BW is an example of organizations that focus on influencing legislation and policy making.

Other religious organizations only serve specific religions, such as Hazon, and some organizations emerge from the religious vision of wealthy philanthropists, such as the Aga Khan Foundation. Hazon is an organization committed to strengthening Jewish life around the world and building a sustainable world for everyone. Hazon's staff and volunteers, as well as the communities they work with, are Jewish and provide programs that deepen Jewish identity and explore the connections among Jewish wisdom, climate, the natural environment, and food. Hazon has numerous projects related to environmental sustainability and food security, with a "particular focus on food systems, because food is central to both Jewish life and our impact in the world." The Aga Khan Foundation (AKF) serves and employs communities and individuals globally from all backgrounds. Founded by His Highness the Aga Khan, 49th hereditary imam of the Shia Ismaili Muslims, the AKF is based in Islam's belief that religious leaders should both interpret the faith for followers and help improve the quality of life for all people. AKF works to reduce inequalities globally and "effectively reduce poverty, ensure tangible food security, and improve the livelihoods of smallholder farmers and their families."

See also: Deforestation; Overpopulation; Sustainability

Further Reading

Choi, Kwan, and Beladi, Hamid. 2016. *Food Security in a Food Abundant World: An Individual Country Perspective*. Bingley, UK: Emerald Publishing Limited.

Collinson, Paul, and Helen M. Macbeth, eds. 2017. *Food in Zones of Conflict: Cross-Disciplinary Perspectives*. New York: Berghahn Books.

Shiva, Vandana. 2016. *Religion and Sustainable Agriculture: World Spiritual Traditions and Food Ethics*. Edited by Todd LeVasseur, Pramod Parajuli, and Norman Wirzba. Lexington: University Press of Kentucky.

Francis of Assisi

Francis of Assisi (ca. 1181–1226), one of the most popular Catholic saints, was born Giovanni di Pietro di Bernardone in Assisi, Italy, around 1181 CE. Born to a wealthy family, as a young adult he had a series of spiritual experiences that inspired him to follow a simple life of poverty, begging, and preaching the Christian Gospel. Francis encouraged his friends and the people of the region to follow his example by preaching enthusiastically in public spaces and imitating the style of jongleurs and troubadours of his time. Francis cofounded several religious organizations, including religious orders that eventually became the Order of Friars Minor (OFM), the Order of Saint Clare, and the Third Order of Saint Francis. Drawing from accounts written by his contemporaries, Francis of Assisi is usually depicted posing peacefully with animals, in religious ecstasy, or acting as a peaceful intermediary during a conflict. Over the centuries, Francis became increasingly associated with a deep love of the natural environment and was formally proclaimed the Catholic Church's patron saint of animals and ecology. In recent times, Francis of Assisi has been an inspiration for global interreligious environmental efforts, such as the 1986 Assisi Declarations, and for official Catholic doctrine, such as Pope Francis I's second encyclical *Laudato Si': On Care of Our Common Home* in 2015.

Based on written accounts of his life, as well as on the stories and songs of itinerant troubadours in medieval Europe, Francis was a mystic, a dedicated peacemaker, and a lover of animals and the natural world. He was also committed to preaching in the language of the people and was deeply concerned for those who were impoverished, ill, or dying. His father was a wealthy cloth merchant based in Assisi, and his mother was from the Provençal region of France, with both providing a sheltered, leisurely life for the young Francis. In his late youth or early adulthood, Francis reportedly suffered a serious illness during which he experienced a spiritual transformation that led to him rejecting his father's wealth and social class. This rejection involved giving some of his father's money to the poor, walking the streets of Assisi barefoot while preaching the Gospel, and ultimately stripping himself naked in front of the bishop of Assisi, who had been attempting to resolve the conflict between Francis and his father.

In the written accounts of Francis's life, there are numerous events reflecting his affinity with all of God's creation and creatures, including his preaching to the birds and his peacemaking with the "wolf of Gubbio," a wolf that terrorized the city of Gubbio and attacked its livestock. The religious song *Canticle of the Creatures*, also known as *Canticle of the Sun*, written by Francis himself, also suggests a deep affinity to the natural environment through praising God, whose glory is described as manifest in the sun, the elements of fire and water, the moon and stars, the wind, "Sister Mother Earth," and "Sister Bodily Death." There exist many stories of Francis as the compassionate friar who rejected wealth in favor of wandering the countryside, interacting with nature, and treating all of God's creatures as spiritual equals, and they have led to his emergence in modern times as an icon of religious environmentalism.

In 1979 Pope John Paul II named Francis of Assisi as the Catholic Church's patron saint of ecology, which formalized the general public perception of Francis as a religious environmentalist. The historian Lynn Townsend White Jr. had made this exact recommendation years earlier, suggesting in 1967 that "Francis be the patron saint of ecology" since the early Franciscans had understood the "spiritual autonomy of all parts of nature." Although the OFM had historically included the love of nature as God's creation as part of their informal organizational culture, in 2003 OFM friars were instructed by OFM leaders to become actively involved in addressing environmental issues.

By 2011 the OFM Office for Justice, Peace, and the Integrity of Creation (JPIC) had focused OFM institutional efforts on environmental justice issues as an intentional reflection of their founder, Francis of Assisi. The Secular Franciscan Order (OFS), comprised of laypersons around the world, has also formally placed environmental justice issues at the center of its work, albeit with an emphasis on individual choices made during daily life. Other Franciscan organizations, such as the numerous and diverse Franciscan women's religious orders and the Franciscan Third

Order Regular, have also committed to incorporating environmental justice into their missions and theological training as an intentional reflection of their founder's charism.

The influence of Francis tends to be strongest in contemporary Christian mission statements on environmental justice, but he is also an icon for spiritually motivated environmentalism in other religious traditions. Some scholars have suggested that Francis was pantheistic or animistic in his religious impulses, but Christian theologians have consistently defined his thought as theocentric, not ecocentric. Contemporary Franciscan theologians are increasingly developing a formal, distinct Franciscan theology of nature based on the charism of Francis of Assisi, his work, and related Christian texts. Additionally, Franciscan orders have been proposing ways for Franciscan academics, Franciscan leaders, Franciscan institutions, and Franciscan communities to embrace a Franciscan theology of nature that can be practiced in their work and daily lives.

In Franciscan theology of nature, humans are seen as part of nature and "enmeshed in the natural world" that is always impacted by human societies. Similarly, human agriculture and technology are seen as potentially destructive to the natural world and must be implemented with great care. As part of this theology of nature, Franciscan academics are asked to consider advanced training in the natural or social sciences, foster interdisciplinary and interreligious scholarship, and serve with organizations such as the Franciscan JPIC, Franciscans International, or the National Religious Partnership for the Environment (NRPE). Contemporary Franciscan leaders are strongly encouraged to promote environmental stewardship and develop environmental advocacy initiatives for their respective orders and for "younger men and women attracted to the Franciscan movement." This practical theology also includes reaching out to secular scientists and public ecologists, with these and all efforts centered on Christian environmental stewardship based on the spirituality of Francis of Assisi.

Francis of Assisi continues to inspire activism, theology, philosophy, organizations, and institutional strategies related to environmentalism. Because it is the birthplace of Francis of Assisi, in 1986 Prince Philip, president of the World Wildlife Fund (WWF) chose Assisi, Italy, as the meeting place for the WWF launching that year of the interreligious Alliance of Religions and Conservation (ARC). As a model of environmental stewardship, Francis was also recognized as providing inspiration for the Assisi Declarations: Messages on Man and Nature from Buddhism,

Christianity, Hinduism, Islam and Judaism, a booklet resulting from the 1986 Assisi meeting.

In addition to references in popular culture and secular environmentalism, Francis is often noted as being the model for current religious doctrine on environmental justice. In the 2015 papal encyclical *Laudato Si': On Care for Our Common Home*, written by Pope Francis I, Francis of Assisi is cited as the inspiration for the document. Pope Francis begins this encyclical by referencing *Canticle of the Creatures* and stating that "Saint Francis of Assisi reminds us that our common home is like a sister with whom we share our life and a beautiful mother who opens her arms to embrace us." Throughout *Laudato Si'*, Pope Francis references the patron saint of ecology, explaining that Francis of Assisi "shows us just how inseparable the bond is between concern for nature, justice for the poor, commitment to society, and interior peace" and "invites us to see nature as a magnificent book in which God speaks to us and grants us a glimpse of his infinite beauty and goodness."

See also: Alliance of Religions and Conservation: Assisi Declarations; Environmental Justice; *Laudato Si'*; National Religious Partnership for the Environment; Pope Francis I; White, Lynn Townsend, Jr.

Further Reading

Armstrong, Edward A. 1973. *Saint Francis: Nature Mystic: The Derivation and Significance of the Nature Stories in the Franciscan Legend.* Berkeley: University of California Press.

Dalarun, Jacques, and Timothy Johnson. 2016. *The Rediscovered Life of St. Francis of Assisi.* Ashland, OH: Franciscan Institute.

Francis, Pope. 2015. *Praise Be to You: Laudato Si': On Care for Our Common Home.* San Francisco: Ignatius Press.

Saggau, Elise. 2003. *Franciscans and Creation: What Is Our Responsibility?* CFIT/ESC-OFM Series: No. 3. St. Bonaventure, NY: Franciscan Institute Publications.

G

Gaia Hypothesis

The Gaia hypothesis was first formulated in the late 1960s by the atmospheric chemist James Lovelock, who named his hypothesis after the Greek goddess who personified Earth. According to the Gaia hypothesis, or Gaia theory, Earth is a living organism that comprises interdependent parts constantly moving toward equilibrium or balance. As a consultant for NASA in the 1960s, Lovelock had been calculating the possibility of life on Mars based on atmospheric composition. In 1971 microbiologist Lynn Margulis began an ongoing collaboration with Lovelock in attempts to develop and scientifically test the Gaia hypothesis. Lovelock and others published several related scientific journal articles in the 1970s, but it was his 1979 book, *Gaia: A New Look at Life on Earth*, that introduced the concept to a broader audience. Responses from the scientific community to Lovelock's Gaia hypothesis were mixed. However, some climate scientists and environmentalists expressed enthusiasm for the theory, and by the 1980s the Gaia hypothesis had become an important part of philosophical and theological discussions in several religious traditions.

Lovelock's initial Gaia hypothesis, based on his observations and research as an atmospheric chemist, include three core assertions about Earth. His basic assertion is that Earth is made up of various living entities and nonliving parts that are all interdependent in a self-regulating system. A second, related assertion is that the planet is in a state of equilibrium, and if anything changes, then it affects the entire system and its parts, resulting in imbalance. Earth can adjust to small changes, but larger changes in the environment can create a new equilibrium that may be hostile to life-forms of the previous state of equilibrium. A third controversial assertion in Lovelock's theory is that Gaia is the largest living creature of

Earth and has organs, such as atmosphere, oceans, wetlands, or rainforests, that are all interdependent and essential to sustaining life.

Additionally, for both Lovelock and his microbiologist colleague Margulis, symbiosis and cooperation among all of Gaia's entities and parts are as important to biological evolution as is competition for survival. In their writing and presentation of Gaia theory, neither Lovelock nor Margulis self-identifies as an environmentalist, nor does either support the idea that humans are the most significant creatures in the self-regulating Gaia organism. Lovelock asserts that Gaia adapts to all changes, including those caused by humans, and can recover even from pollution or nuclear war.

By the 1980s there were both philosophical and theological responses to the Gaia hypothesis, with some having a clear influence on religiously motivated environmentalism. In 1987 the World Council of Churches (WCC) convened meetings in Amsterdam to discuss the ecological crisis. Lovelock attended those meetings and discussed the Gaia hypothesis with theologians and religious leaders, including Protestant theologian Douglas John Hall. One of the results of these meetings was a discussion paper by Hall and Lovelock titled "Reintegrating God's Creation," which integrates themes from the Gaia hypothesis into a theological commentary on the destructive ecological habits of humans, as well as their potentially healing roles as stewards, priests, and poets of Earth.

In the 1990s several works published by prominent theologians explicitly incorporated elements of the Gaia hypothesis. These works include Rosemary Radford Ruether's *Gaia and God: An Ecofeminist Theology of Earth-Healing* and Thomas Berry's synthesis of Christian theology and science, *The Universe Story: From the Primordial Flaring Forth to the Ecozoic Era*. Although the initial theological responses in the 1980s were mostly from Christian thinkers, by the twenty-first century, concepts and themes inspired by the Gaia hypothesis were present in the ecotheological writings of many religions and in the rhetoric of religious environmental activists.

Lovelock continued to personify Earth as Gaia in his later works, including *The Revenge of Gaia: Why the Earth is Fighting Back* (2006) and *The Vanishing Face of Gaia: A Final Warning* (2009). However, he clearly explains that the concept of Gaia has always been a metaphor or vehicle for his scientific thought and that he has never believed Earth to be an actual, sentient organism. Nonetheless, both contemporary philosophers and theologians credit Lovelock with both initiating a discussion of the planet as a unified, integrated whole, and inspiring religious adherents to envision a divine creation made of interdependent entities and elements. Many contemporary scholars credit Lovelock with creating a synthesis of science, mysticism, religion, and environmentalism, and the Gaia hypothesis continues to appear in works ranging from Latter-day Saints' writings on environmental stewardship to research on British Eco-Pagans, as well as numerous other studies addressing religion, religious belief, ecology, and environmentalism.

See also: Ecofeminism; Ecotheology; Teilhard de Chardin, Pierre; World Council of Churches

Further Reading

Lovelock, James. 1995. *Gaia: A New Look at Life on Earth.* Oxford: Oxford University Press.

Ruether, Rosemary Radford. 1992. *Gaia and God: An Ecofeminist Theology of Earth Healing.* San Francisco: Harper San Francisco.

Swimme, Brian, and Thomas Mary Berry. 1992. *The Universe Story: From the Primordial Flaring Forth to the Ecozoic Era—A Celebration of the Unfolding of the Cosmos.* New York: HarperCollins Publishers.

Green Pilgrimage Network

The Green Pilgrimage Network (GPN) is a global interfaith project connecting pilgrim cities, routes, and sites that embrace religiously motivated environmentalism. The GPN was launched in 2011 in Assisi, Italy, under the auspices of the Alliance of Religions and Conservation (ARC). GPN's original goal was to bring together religious, political, and economic organizations and individuals to raise environmental awareness, reduce the negative environmental impact of pilgrimage sites and routes, and to enhance pilgrims' experience through interaction with the natural world. GPN became independent from ARC by 2015 and changed its name to the European Green Pilgrimage Network (EGPN), which collaborates with sacred sites and communities around the world as well as world-level organizations such as the United Nations. EPGN, still generally referred to as the Green Pilgrimage Network, is involved in environmentally friendly activities that benefit religious pilgrims and the sacred sites they visit.

The GPN includes pilgrimage sites and communities in China, India, Europe, Africa, the Americas, and the Middle East, and has representation in several different religious traditions, including Christianity, Confucianism, Daoism, Hinduism, Islam, Sikhism, Shinto, and Baha'ism. Many of these pilgrimage sites are designated as World Heritage Sites by the United Nations Educational, Scientific and Cultural Organization (UNESCO). Additionally, the United Nations World Tourism Organization (UNWTO), which views environmentally friendly religious pilgrimage as a type of cultural, economic, and political development, has its own Green Pilgrimage Project that focuses on religious pilgrimage as an important segment of the travel industry. Both UNESCO and UNWTO work with politicians and other stakeholders who are interested in creating jobs and economic growth along pilgrim routes. Some of their growth strategies include using low-impact tourism that accommodates religious pilgrims, strengthening local traditions, and providing pilgrims with access to twenty-first-century digital technology.

The GPN shares several goals and strategies with UNESCO and UNWTO for globally developing green pilgrimage. These organizations have collaborated on identifying pilgrimage objectives, assessing the economic impact of pilgrimage, and helping communities develop green pilgrimage plans that facilitate sustainable growth. The UN organizations provide professional assistance in several areas, including policy and program evaluation, connecting stakeholders to regional expertise in tourism management, and marketing green pilgrimage as "socially responsible outdoor activity." Green pilgrimage communities, located near sacred sites or on religious pilgrimage routes, develop green infrastructure, including buildings, energy, water resources and waste management, and also use environmentally friendly transportation. Additionally, these communities pledge to offer "greener and kinder food" and actively promote policies dedicated to the conservation of land, biodiversity, and wilderness. Communities who formally join the GPN pledge to transform "our pilgrim city, place or route into a green, sustainable model in keeping with the beliefs of our faith or the faiths of our pilgrimage place" and work with both "faith and secular groups together to work in partnership towards this vision."

See also: Alliance of Religions and Conservation

Further Reading

Alliance of Religions and Conservation. 2014. *Green Pilgrimage Network: A Handbook for Faith Leaders, Cities, Towns, and Pilgrims.* Bath, UK: ARC.

Greening of Religion Hypothesis

The greening of religion hypothesis (GRH), which examines the general assumption that the world's religions are increasingly involved in environmentalism, was initially proposed in 2011 by Bron Taylor, a professor of religious studies at the University of Florida. This hypothesis is used to test claims that Taylor asserts are made by scholars involved in an academic "religion and ecology movement" that has supported religious environmentalism since the 1990s. Taylor describes the religion and ecology movement as both an academic field of study and an ecumenical religious movement that is a distinct part of the broader religious environmental movement that emerged at the end of the twentieth century. According to Taylor, to understand both the role of religion in environmentalism and to what extent the "greening of religion" is occurring, scholars must state claims that can be tested with research and data. Taylor's hypothesis is an attempt to summarize, formulate, and test claims in existing research on the relationship between religions and environmentalism.

To formulate specific claims for his hypothesis, Taylor reviewed existing research on religion and ecology, religion and environmentalism, and numerous related topics. In "The Greening of Religion Hypothesis (Part One)," Taylor (2016) identified three consistent claims in the existing research: "Religious ideas are important drivers of environment-impacting behaviors; the world's religions have ideas that can spur environmentally friendly behavior and increasingly are doing so; and green religions are critically important in the quest for environmentally sustainable societies" (296). To test these claims and the general claim that the world's religions are becoming increasingly environmentally friendly, Taylor and others reviewed research and scholarly activities from the 1960s to 2016. Additionally, they determined that the reviewed material fell into four genres: hortatory (encouraging ethical behavior), historical, qualitative, and quantitative. Taylor and his colleagues also noted that (1) there was no consensus on the definition or function of religion, (2) there was a lack of research on the correlations between political attitudes and environmentalism of religious believers, and (3) much of the research erroneously presented findings from single case studies as representative of entire religious traditions.

Taylor found that while existing research indicates that religious ideas can hinder environmental action, the claims of scholars, such as Lynn Townsend White Jr., about the specific culpability of Judeo-Christian traditions in environmental destruction were not supported. Taylor and his colleagues also noted that much of the existing research on religious environmentalism prior to 2016 covers Christianity in the United States, so there was not enough research to support claims of increased environmentally friendly behavior in the world's religions. Regarding the third claim in the hypothesis, Taylor acknowledged that some religious organizations are politically engaged with environmental issues, such as the Islamic Foundation for Ecology and Environmental Sciences (IFEES) and the Evangelical Environmental Network (EEN), but noted that these organizations are not necessarily representative of an entire religious tradition's approach to environmental issues. The existing research also suggested that religion and theological views are not consistent predictors of environmentally friendly attitudes and behaviors, so it is unclear if the role of "green religion" is critical in creating environmentally sustainable societies.

Taylor's GRH represents one of the first efforts to provide a social-scientific model for collecting and testing data on the rise of religious environmentalism and the role of religiously motivated individuals, organizations, and communities in shaping public environmental policy. Additionally, Taylor's broad definition of religion creates opportunities for an expanded understanding of religious environmentalism and encourages research ranging on a spectrum from predominant world religions to obscure "religious-resembling" communities. Although the primary purpose of the GRH was to identify and test claims in existing research, it also provides a method for understanding the specifics of religiously motivated environmentalism as well as how, in general, individuals, organizations, and communities are mobilized around environmental issues.

See also: Evangelical Environmental Network; Islamic Foundation for Ecology and Environmental Sciences; Religious Environmental Movement; White, Lynn Townsend, Jr.

Further Reading

Taylor, Bron. 2016. "The Greening of Religion Hypothesis (Part One)." *Journal for the Study of Religion, Nature & Culture* 10 (3): 268–305.

Taylor, Bron, Gretel Van Wieren, and Bernard Zaleha. 2016. "The Greening of Religion Hypothesis (Part Two)." *Journal for the Study of Religion, Nature & Culture* 10 (3): 306–78.

Hinduism

Hinduism is an Indian religion comprised of numerous cultural traditions, practices, beliefs, and philosophies that emerged several thousand years ago from the Indus River Valley region near modern Pakistan. Although within Hinduism there are several different theologies and traditions, all adherents of Hinduism share a cosmology, sacred texts, pilgrimage sites, and a core set of practices and rituals. The Vedas and the Upanishads, which include the Bhagavad Gita and other texts, provide the core teachings for all Hindus, with some texts possibly dating back more than four thousand years ago and written in the ancient Indian language of Sanskrit. Although Hinduism has many religious subcultures, there are four major traditions or denominations: Shivaism, which is the reverence of Shiva; Shaktism, which reveres many goddesses as aspects of the Supreme Goddess; Vaishnavism, which reveres Vishnu as the Supreme Lord; and Smartism, which rejects sectarianism and reveres the major deities equally.

Even though there are many traditions and beliefs within Hinduism, there are some basic shared beliefs in (1) a Supreme Being who is creator of all things, (2) the divine nature of the Vedas, (3) karma as the law of cause and effect, (4) the idea that the universe is created and dissolved in endless cycles, (5) transmigration of the soul until karma is resolved, (6) the possibility of communion with deities through rituals and devotionals, (7) the practice of ahimsa or nonviolence in words and actions, (8) and the idea that all religions offer a path to God or the Transcendent Absolute. Currently there are around 1.2 billion adherents of Hinduism globally, mostly in the Asia-Pacific region, including India, with significant numbers of Hindu communities found throughout the rest of the world.

For centuries there have been several consistent teachings based on Vedic sacred texts that explain the relationships among the universe, the

71

natural world, and all life, including humans. Although many variations exist, the core concepts used to explain the relationship between humans and the natural world include *ishavasyam*, the *web of life*, *ahimsa*, *karma*, and *reincarnation*, or the cycle of rebirth. *Ishavasyam* is the belief that the Supreme God or Transcendent Absolute is omnipresent and resides in infinite forms, including all life throughout and within the natural environment. Space, air, fire, water, and earth are the five great elements, known as the *pancha mahabhutas*, that interweave to create a *web of life*. This web of life interconnects all life, with the five great elements all emanating from prakriti, the primal energy that is the essence of all matter.

The core concept of ahimsa, or nonviolence, is considered the most important duty, or dharma, of humans and creates positive karma. Caring for and loving the earth, including all life in the natural environment, is an aspect of ahimsa and improves a person's karma, as does a vegetarian diet. Another core concept is the cycle of rebirth, or reincarnation, in which every being experiences rebirth through many cycles in many different forms; it has for centuries been a core belief, and it teaches that all species are interconnected throughout time and across forms. Historically Hinduism and the ancient Vedic traditions have understood the relationship between humans and the natural world through these and other core concepts and beliefs, which continue to be reinterpreted with each new generation and constantly changing social contexts.

Hinduism has traditionally viewed nature as sacred and part of the web of life, and some contemporary scholars have suggested that it is inherently environmentalist. However, Hinduism and Vedic philosophy have tended to emphasize that problems in the material world are to be transcended rather than resolved through organized social action. There are exceptions, such as the Bishnoi community, founded in the 1400s, whose culture prohibits the cutting of trees and killing of animals and who inspired the modern Chipko movement that emerged in India in the 1970s. Such rural communities that practice sustainability, protect their ecosystem, and believe in the interconnectedness of all life do not necessarily consider themselves to be social activists but instead usually frame their environmentally friendly and sustainable lifestyles as their dharma, rooted in thousands of years of Vedic and pre-Vedic culture.

Although the web of life and the sanctity of the natural world are important beliefs in Hinduism, and many traditional rural communities have put these beliefs into practice for centuries, contemporary adherents of Hinduism have just begun to express their traditional beliefs as a religious environmental movement that shares goals with the secular environmental movement. Mohandas Gandhi, one of the most significant world leaders of the twentieth century, made the Hindu concept of nonviolence (ahimsa) the foundation of the Indian independence movement, and he inspired future generations to merge elements of Hinduism and Jainism with environmentalism and civil rights activism. Similarly, the activism of the Indian physicist and environmental activist Vandana Shiva is a contemporary example of how individuals merge traditional Hinduism with the secular environmental movement. Vandana Shiva became interested in environmental activism in the 1970s through India's Chipko movement. Shiva references ancient Vedic texts that teach about the sacred gifts of the earth, describes her activism as dharma that supports biodiversity and the web of life, and anchors her ecofeminism and current environmental justice projects in Hinduism as well as Gandhian ideals.

Brahma Vidya Mandir (BVM), an intentional community for women in central India along the Dham River, is also anchored in Vedic and Gandhian ideals. In 1959, Vinoba Bhave established BVM as an ashram committed to nonviolence and justice for the poor. Although devoted to Vedic spirituality and adherence to Hindu religious culture, BVM differs from most ashrams in that it is also involved in social change activism and related local, regional, and global outreach. BVM resists industrial agriculture and monoculture, instead advocating for biodiversity of foods and seeds, practicing nonviolence and equality, and supporting local farmers. As of 2019 BVM was home to around thirty women, with an extended community that includes farmers and villagers from the region as well as visitors interested in sustainability and nonviolence. All BVM residents practice daily communal recitation from sacred texts, including the Ishavasya Upanishad, Vishnu-Sahasranama, and the Bhagavad Gita.

In addition to ashram communities focusing on environmental issues, adherents of Hinduism concerned with India's sacred rivers are merging traditional Vedic concepts and practices with modern social movement strategies. Since the 1990s several efforts committed to protecting and preserving sacred rivers have gained force, including the Save Ganga movement and similar nonprofit organizations that focus on the Yamuna and other rivers. The Yamuna River is one of the largest tributaries of the Ganges River and is revered by many adherents of Hinduism because it has traditionally been associated with Lord Krishna, the incarnation of Vishnu. Despite this sacred association, the Yamuna is considered one of the world's most polluted and ecologically dead rivers due to fertilizers, pesticides, sewage, and industrial waste. For several decades, religiously motivated environmental activists have worked to bring this river system back to life.

In 2017, in response to pressure by religious activists, nonprofit organizations, and regional governmental agencies, the Indian state of Uttarakhand awarded to the Yamuna and Ganges Rivers "all corresponding rights, duties and liabilities of a living person," which many expect will bring the rivers back to life over time. Although many individuals and organizations have contributed, the most effective environmental activism on behalf of Hinduism's sacred rivers has been the Save Ganga movement, started in 1998 by the National Women's Organization (NWO) in Pune, India. In accordance with NWO's primary mission of the protection of nature and women, the Save Ganga movement seeks to replace the "eco-hostile culture of development" with a culture based on nonviolence (ahimsa). The Save Ganga movement also provided inspiration for Prime Minister Narendra Modi's Clean Ganges Project, which committed to the revitalization of religious tourism with the promise that the Ganges River "will be clean by 2020."

Collaboration is an important and effective strategy for addressing environmental issues. Recognizing this, Hindu religious leaders and adherents from India and around the world have been involved with inter-religious efforts to address climate change. In 2009, Hindu spiritual and religious leaders submitted the first Hindu Declaration on Climate Change, at the Parliament of the World's Religions. The 2009 Declaration states that Hindus believe "the earth, the water, the fire, the air and space—as well as the various orders of life, including plants and trees, forests and animals, are bound to each other within life's cosmic web." However, it argues that humanity has not applied these beliefs and "centuries of rapacious exploitation of the planet have caught up with us, and a radical change in our relationship with nature is no longer an option. It is matter of survival." It also states that Gandhi would have insisted that Hindus "take the lead in Earth-friendly living, personal frugality, lower power consumption, alternative energy, sustainable food production and vegetarianism," all of which affect climate change.

In 2015 another Hindu Declaration on Climate Change was submitted to the United Nations Framework Convention on Climate Change (UNFCCC) in preparation and support for the Paris Agreement. Climate change is defined as a problem for all of creation: "Ether, air, fire, water, earth, planets, all creatures, directions, trees and plants, rivers and seas, they are all organs of God's body. Remembering this a devotee respects all species" (Śrīmad Bhāgavatam 11.2.41). The 2015 Declaration more clearly explains Hindu environmental ethics, and it references numerous sacred texts that inform those ethics, while the 2009 Declaration is a brief, general statement with reference to Gandhi and some Hindu concepts.

The environmental work of Hindu leaders and activists, collaborating with the UN, Parliament of the World's Religions, and the Alliance of Religions and Conservation (ARC), has provided a framework for religious environmentalism among Hindus around the world. Inspired by organizations such as the ARC and several UN environmental initiatives, the Bhumi Project began in 2009 at the Oxford Centre for Hindu Studies in collaboration with GreenFaith, an international interfaith coalition. The Bhumi Project is representative of Hinduism's global involvement in environmentalism and has several ongoing projects including Compassionate Living, Hindu Environment Week, the Green Temple, Prana Healthcare for All, and numerous sponsored events each year. Developed both for Hindus and the general public, these ongoing projects provide guidance for engaging in religious environmentalism, such as recommendations for cruelty-free living, creating green worship spaces in homes and temples, and volunteer opportunities for health-care professionals. The 2019 "Hindu Earth Ethics and Climate Action" conference, attended by Hindu theologians, community activists, and environmental scholars, is a recent example of events sponsored and organized by the Bhumi Project. The conference covered climate activism, the history of faith-based environmentalism, and how young Hindus could become and/or were involved in environmental activism.

Going back thousands of years, Hinduism has taught that the natural environment is a web of life, in which everything is connected, and the Supreme God or Transcendent Absolute is present in each creature and the natural elements. The Hindu concept of reincarnation, in which all living things experience rebirth in a variety of forms, is also inseparable from Hindu understandings of the natural environment. Although Hinduism for centuries has taught that all life and the earth itself should be respected and treated with compassion, it is only within recent decades that a distinctly Hindu environmental movement has developed. As followers of Hinduism and Vedic philosophy combine traditional practices and beliefs with secular environmentalism, they are discovering new ways to express their religious values. In some cases, religiously motivated environmentalism has been able to influence political leaders and shape national and international environmental policies. In other examples, small religious communities such as ashrams have merged ascetic lifestyles with global outreach on environmental issues.

See also: Alliance of Religions and Conservation; Assisi Declarations; Jainism; Paris Agreement; Religious Environmental Movement; Shiva, Vandana.

Further Reading

Drew, Georgina. 2017. *River Dialogues: Hindu Faith and the Political Ecology of Dams on the Sacred Ganga.* Tucson: University of Arizona Press.

Jain, Pankaj. 2016. *Dharma and Ecology of Hindu Communities: Sustenance and Sustainability.* London: Routledge.

Kent, Eliza F. 2013. *Sacred Groves and Local Gods: Religion and Environmentalism in South India.* New York: Oxford University Press.

Nelson, Lance E. 1998. *Purifying the Earthly Body of God: Religion and Ecology in Hindu India.* Albany: State University of New York Press.

Ramachandran, R. 2018. *A History of Hinduism: The Past, Present, and Future.* New Delhi and Thousand Oaks, CA: Sage.

Subramaniam, Banu. 2019. *Holy Science: The Biopolitics of Hindu Nationalism.* Seattle: University of Washington Press.

Hydraulic Fracturing

Hydraulic fracturing is a drilling method that injects fluids into the ground to facilitate the extraction of petroleum, shale gas, coal bed methane, or other resources trapped in bedrock and other subterranean natural reservoirs. Commonly referred to as "fracking," this process injects water, chemicals, and sand at high pressure through a well system into the ground, which fractures and widens cracks in bedrock, releasing petroleum or gas, and forcing it out of the rock and back up through the well system. Petroleum and natural gas extraction companies are increasingly using fracking techniques in their operations around the world, including locations in Australia, New Zealand, Africa, Canada, the United States, the United Kingdom, China, and Europe. Although fracking has increased oil production and decreased petroleum prices, it has become increasingly controversial in the twenty-first century due to its destructive environmental impacts. A few of the negative environmental impacts include methane leaks and other toxic emissions, water contamination, excessive use of water, earthquakes, and health risks, which have been shown to disproportionally affect Indigenous and rural communities.

In the early twenty-first century, religiously and spiritually motivated groups began protesting fracking, including Indigenous people, rural communities, and adherents of nature religions. Often these fracking protests are focused on the local or regional risks experienced by communities that share religious or spiritual beliefs, rather than on fracking as a global issue. For example, Aboriginal people have mobilized to protect their sacred ancestral lands in remote regions of Australia, where energy companies are expanding their shale gas fracking operations. In the United States, Lumbee Indians and rural African American communities have opposed the Atlantic Coast Pipeline that is part of a fracking operation that moves methane gas six hundred miles across their sacred lands and homelands in the state of North Carolina. Similarly, the Texas Society of Native Nations has protested the Jupiter and Kinder Morgan Pipelines in Texas and Louisiana, which incorporate fracking operations, and the Standing Rock Sioux continue to protest against the Dakota Access Pipeline system that transports oil from the Bakken Shale fracking operations to corporate markets across the United States.

When compared with the world's major religions, adherents of numerous Indigenous spiritual paths, Paganism, and other nature religions are more likely to actively oppose any activity that destroys the natural environment. Adherents of Paganism, such as Druids and Wiccans, hold public rituals and participate in direct action protests that oppose fracking because it damages the natural environment and poses health risks for all species. Communities within the world's major religions are also involved in fracking issues, although their support varies. Some, such as Christians in the Kamoo region of South Africa, support fracking for the economic benefits it brings, and others, such as Lutheran Christian churches in the United States, oppose fracking because of the harm it causes the natural environment and rural communities. Overall, adherents of major world religions such as Buddhism, Christianity, Hinduism, Islam, and Judaism tend to oppose fracking but are not as united in their opposition as are Indigenous communities and adherents of Paganism and nature religions.

See also: Energy; Nature Religions; Paganism; Pollution; Water

Further Reading

Gamper-Rabindran, Shanti, ed. 2018. *The Shale Dilemma: A Global Perspective on Fracking and Shale Development*. Pittsburgh, PA: University of Pittsburgh Press.

Sernovitz, Gary. 2016. *The Green and the Black: The Complete Story of the Shale Revolution, the Fight Over Fracking, and the Future of Energy*. New York: St. Martin's Press.

I

Interfaith Power and Light

Interfaith Power and Light (IPL) is an interfaith nonprofit organization that helps faith communities become socially and politically engaged in fighting global warming. Originally founded as Episcopal Power and Light in 1997 by Rev. Sally Bingham and Episcopalians in California, the group changed its name in 2000 to California Interfaith Power and Light and then again in 2001 to Interfaith Power and Light. As IPL expanded, it became part of the broader Regeneration Project, which is an interfaith ministry dedicated to addressing environmental issues and impacting related public policy. With the help of IPL, religious communities across the United States have formed IPL organizations in their regions, with many registering as nonprofits. More than twenty thousand congregations across the United States have joined IPL, which works with each congregation to develop energy stewardship programs fitted to their specific regional and community needs.

Although IPL campaigns and programs are national, each of the local or regional IPL organizations decides how to participate and how a program should be implemented. For example, IPL's Faith Climate Action Week is locally planned to coincide annually in April with Earth Day, and the Cool Congregations program provides guidance for congregations who want to combat global warming by making changes in their homes and places of worship. Other IPL programs that are locally designed and implemented include Cool Harvest, which helps congregations educate members about climate-friendly food choices and activities such as organic gardening, and Carbon Covenant, which provides support to faith communities involved in halting deforestation. Other examples of IPL campaigns are Faith to Ford, which petitioned Ford Corporation to support clean energy policies, and building support in faith communities for the

Green New Deal in U.S. politics. Although IPL is involved in international conferences, policies, and campaigns, its primary focus is helping U.S. religious congregations impact U.S. environmental policy through the types of local and regional activities described above.

IPL has been critical of U.S. environmental policy, and in 2017 created the "Paris: We're Still In" campaign in response to the United States withdrawing from the United Nations' Paris Agreement on Climate Change. In this campaign, individuals and congregations affiliated with IPL pledged that they would continue to work to protect the environment, which they define as God's creation, regardless of governmental policies or action. In 2017 IPL publicly opposed U.S. president Trump's Executive Order 13783, "Promoting Energy Independence and Economic Growth." IPL claimed that Executive Order 13783 reverses U.S. policies aimed at reliable, affordable, and renewable energy and impedes any related improvements in air and water quality. In 2019 IPL objected to the appointment of former coal lobbyist Andrew Wheeler as U.S. Environmental Protection Agency (EPA) administrator. IPL asserted that because of Andrew Wheeler's association with the coal industry, he would likely reverse or eliminate existing EPA clean energy policies.

See also: Climate Change; Paris Agreement

Further Reading

McDuff, Mallory. 2014. *Sacred Acts: How Churches Are Working to Protect Earth's Climate*. Gabriola Island, Canada: New Society.

Islam

Islam is a monotheistic religion that emerged in the early seventh century in the western region of Arabia. Islam is one of the three Abrahamic religions, along with Christianity and Judaism, and the most recent one to emerge, with Muhammad ibn Abdullah al-Hashimi of Mecca (ca. 570–632 CE) as the final prophet of God (Allah). From age forty until his death, Muhammad received divine revelations that became the Qur'an, which is believed by Muslims to be the word of God (Allah) and provides the foundation for Islamic beliefs and practices. Although the Qur'an is the ultimate and uncorrupted word of God for Muslims, the Torah, the Psalms, and the Gospel, which are mentioned in the Qur'an, are also believed to be the word of God as revealed to Moses, David, and Jesus. Additionally, the Hadith, which are the collected accounts of Muhammad's words and deeds as the last prophet of Islam, provide examples for how to live as a Muslim. Mentioned in the Qur'an and the Hadith, the Five Pillars of Islam are belief, prayer, charity, fasting during Ramadan, and pilgrimage, and are practiced by Muslims around the world. In 2015 the world's Muslim population was estimated at more than 1.8 billion, with around 80 percent living in Asia, the Middle East, and North Africa and the remainder of Muslim communities located in all of the world's inhabited continents.

The Qur'an provides the foundation for Muslims' beliefs about the natural world. In the Qur'an, God is identified as the creator of everything, humans are named as stewards of the earth, human corruption and waste are condemned, and all forms of life are inherently valued as God's creation. Because all creatures and life are a sign and a reflection of God, humans must respect and care for them out of love for God. Humans are God's appointed stewards (*khalifah*) and, as God's representatives on earth, are commanded to live in responsible and sustainable ways. Although God grants humans the right to use the animals, plants, and the elements of the earth to meet their needs, they are instructed to do so with justice and mercy. In the Qur'an, humans are told that God "has made you successors upon the Earth and has raised some of you above others in degrees that He may try you through what He has given you" (Qur'an 6:156). Regarding their rank, humans are also told that "there is no creature on or within the earth or bird that flies with its wings except that they are communities like you" (Qur'an 6:38). Additionally, humans must respect the earth as a habitat for all life and as created by God: "The heaven He raised and imposed the balance that you not transgress within the balance. Establish weight in justice and do not make deficient the balance. The Earth He laid out for the creatures" (Qur'an 55: 5–10).

Although the Qur'an has defined and guided Muslims' relationship to the natural environment for centuries, and scholars of Islam were explicitly addressing environmental issues in the 1960s, Muslims did not organize a specifically Islamic environmental movement until the 1990s. In 1966 Seyyed Hossein Nasr, professor of Islamic studies and Islamic philosopher, addressed the current ecological crisis as the spiritual crisis of modern humankind. In a series of University of Chicago lectures, and later in his book, *Man and Nature: The Spiritual Crisis of Modern Man* (1967), Nasr asserted that humanity no longer recognized the spiritual significance of nature and was committing a crime against God by not protecting and respecting creation.

During the 1980s Muslim philosophers, scholars, and activists increasingly noted that there were shared values between Islam and modern environmentalism. Also in the 1980s, leaders in Islam contributed to the founding of the Alliance of Religions and Conservation (ARC) and were regular contributors to United Nations (UN) cultural and religious programs. By 1990s the earlier work of Nasr and others had influenced Muslims around the world, and Muslim scholars in the Arab world, the United Kingdom, and North America began framing environmental issues as part of a spiritual crisis that called for a response from all Muslims. By the 1990s Muslim communities had formed numerous organizations dedicated to addressing environmental issues and stewardship from a distinctly Muslim perspective, based in Qur'an texts that explicitly identify humans as caretakers of God's creation. Representative of this trend, the Islamic Foundation for Ecology and Environmental Sciences (IFEES) was founded in England by Fazlun Khalid in 1994, with other organizations forming since then in Muslim communities around the world.

In the twenty-first century, the term *eco-Islam* is often used in reference to Islamic environmentalism based in the Qur'an and the Hadith. The beginnings of eco-Islam can be traced to the work of Nasr and other Islamic philosophers, as well as to the initiatives of organizational leaders such as IFEES's Khalid. In eco-Islam, environmentally friendly and ecologically sustainable lifestyles are seen as a Muslim obligation, and following these lifestyles and Qur'an-based environmental ethics will help lead humanity out of the current environmental crisis. The natural environment is both a gift and a responsibility given to humans by God, and so all humans, at the individual, community, and societal levels, are obligated to protect and preserve this gift for all creatures and for future generations.

Eco-Islam also teaches that Muslims should refrain from any behaviors that might harm the natural environment or disrupt the balance created by God. The Qur'an, as well as the actions and words of Muhammad in the Hadith, provide the three concepts and principles of *tawhid, khalifah*, and *maslahah* that define the relationships among God, the natural environment, and humans. Tawhid, which refers to the oneness or unity of God, is the most important belief in Islam, and in Eco-Islamic environmentalism is the basis for requiring that humans always seek balance or sustainability in their relationship with the natural environment. The concept of *khalifah* refers to humans' role as stewards of the natural environment as appointed by God, and it requires that Muslims protect the earth for current and future generations. Maslahah, which is the Islamic concept of public good, is interpreted in Islamic environmentalism as the requirement that each Muslim must prevent harm to the natural environment, which was created by God to sustain all life.

Islamic environmentalism, following eco-Islamic or other models, is being put into practice by a growing number of organizations. IFEES was one of the original Islamic environmental organizations that developed approaches to environmental issues and natural resource management, provided training programs, developed and sponsored projects, and established networks of scholars, scientists, and activists. Through these early networks, other leaders and organizations emerged and now participate as Islamic environmentalists in global organizations such as the UN or develop national and regional nodes of environmentalism.

In 2018 Odeh Al-Jayyousi, a professor at Arabian Gulf University, sustainability scholar, and member of the UN Global Scientific Advisory Panel, suggested that Islamic environmentalism's focus on justice and harmony between humans and nature provides useful insights that can help transition societies to sustainable development. Al-Jayyousi proposed addressing climate change and sustainability using a model comprised of green activism (green jihad), green innovation (green ijtihad), and green lifestyle (green zohd). Given that almost 25 percent of the world's population are Muslim, proposals such as Al-Jayyousi's could help numerous communities around the world adopt sustainable lifestyles.

Khaleafa.com, a Canadian organization with international outreach, also sees Islamic environmentalism as offering a model that can have global impact. One of Khaleafa's ongoing projects is the Three C Climate Plan, focused on curbing consumption, conserving energy, and commuting smarter. Recently, Khaleafa's 2019 Green Khutbah campaign worked with religious leaders to deliver *khutbah* (sermons) that teach Muslims how to become responsible stewards of the natural environment.

As a global institution, Islam has regularly issued official statements on environmental issues since at least the 1980s as part of interreligious and international collaborations. In 1986 the Muslim Declaration on Nature was drafted at Assisi, Italy, as part of the Assisi Declarations written by religious leaders and published through the World Wildlife Fund (WWF) and the ARC. A decade later, the 1995 Islamic Faith Statement on Nature was written by Hyder Ihsan Mahasneh of the Muslim World League and submitted to ARC and the World Bank. At the 2012 United Nations

Conference on Environment and Development, also known as the Rio Earth Summit, the Islamic Declaration on Sustainable Development was drafted at the Islamic Conference of Environment Ministers and approved by the Islamic Educational Scientific and Culture Organization. Numerous statements continue to be submitted on both Islamic environmentalism and Islamic positions specific to environmental issues. In 2015 the Islamic Declaration on Global Climate Change was drafted at the International Islamic Climate Change Symposium and made available to all Muslims and the general public.

See also: Alliance of Religions and Conservation; Assisi Declarations; Islamic Foundation for Ecology and Environmental Sciences; Religious Environmental Movement

Further Reading

Abdul-Matin, Ibrahim, and Keith Ellison. 2010. *Green Deen: What Islam Teaches About Protecting the Planet*. San Francisco: Berrett-Koehler.

Ghazi bin Muhammad, Aftab Ahmed, and Reza Shah-Kazemi. 2010. *The Holy Qur'an and the Environment*. Amman, Jordan: Royal Aal al-Bayt Institute for Islamic Thought.

Hancock, Rosemary. 2018. *Islamic Environmentalism: Activism in the United States and Great Britain*. Abingdon, UK: Routledge.

Nasr, Seyyed Hossein. 1967. *The Encounter of Man and Nature: The Spiritual Crisis of Modern Man*. London: Allen & Unwin.

Islamic Foundation for Ecology and Environmental Sciences

The Islamic Foundation for Ecology and Environmental Sciences (IFEES) is an Islamic environmentalist organization based in the United Kingdom that is recognized as being the first international organization of its kind. The primary goal of IFEES is to develop approaches to environmental issues and natural resource management that are based in the Qur'an, Hadith literature, and Islamic values. IFEES activities include providing training programs, developing and sponsoring projects, and establishing networks of scholars, scientists, and activists. The founder of IFEES, Fazlun Khalid, approached conservation and environmental issues from an international, multilingual, multicultural, and Islamic perspective, an approach that continues in the organization in the twenty-first century.

IFEES emerged as a network of Muslim environmental activists, scientists, and scholars in the 1980s and was formally recognized as a UK charity in 1994. Members of this network contributed to publications and projects sponsored by the World Wide Fund for Nature (formally World Wildlife Fund [WWF]) and Alliance of Religions and Conservation (ARC), as well as to those of other international, nongovernmental organizations. Although IFEES members participated in both international, governmental and nongovernmental organizations, they continued to focus on providing Muslims around the world with practical solutions to environmental problems based on scientific research and Islamic values. Beginning in the 1990s, IFEES published essays such as "Ecology, Sustainability, and Future Generations: An Islamic Perspective" (1997) and "The Tree and the Forest: An Islamic Perspective" (1999), and a training manual on "Qur'an, Creation and Conservation" (1999). In the 2000s IFEES members published and presented on Islamic approaches to animal advocacy, fashion and sustainability, globalization, forest conservation, global warming, and many other related topics, as well as distributing the newsletter *EcoIslam* and educational materials such as the *Muslim Green Guide to Reducing Climate Change*. Educational materials, publications, and presentations by IFEES are aimed at several Muslim audiences ranging in age, education level, profession, and interest.

IFEES takes complex scientific studies and makes them accessible to the general Muslim population in many regions around the world. The mission of IFEES is to connect Muslims' religious values to their local, regional, and global environmental issues, and enable them to take action that is grounded both in science and in Islamic values. Additionally, IFEES organizes and provides support for local events that encourage Muslims to engage in environmentalism and civil discourse in their communities, with governments, and with other religious traditions. As an organization, IFEES has engaged in the strategic use of social media internet platforms to provide frequent updates on events, decisions, funding, and issues of interest to Muslim environmentalists and Islamic organizations around the world. Through social media and current event updates, IFEES continues to encourage and prepare Muslim environmentalists for outreach and effective political engagement. For example, in 2015 IFEES members in Samoa issued a formal request for political leaders around the world to stop human causes of climate change, and in 2019 British members participated in the UK Climate Coalition. Similarly, since 2015, IFEES members have been involved globally in implementing Green Mosques, reduced use of plastics, and recycling practices.

See also: Alliance of Religions and Conservation; Islam; Religious Environmental Movement

Further Reading

Hancock, Rosemary. 2017. *Islamic Environmentalism: Activism in the United States and Great Britain.* London: Taylor & Francis.

Khaled, Amr, and Fazlun Khalid. 2008. *Muslim Green Guide to Reducing Climate Change.* Birmingham, UK: Islamic Foundation for Ecology and Environmental Sciences, and LifeMakers UK.

J

Jainism

Jainism is a religion that emerged in India around 500 BCE. Its origins are in the teachings of Mahavira, a member of a royal dynasty and the warrior caste, who lived around this same time in the northeastern region of India. The Jain religion currently is estimated to have between four million and ten million followers globally, mostly in India, with some members living in temples as monks or nuns, and others practicing their beliefs as laypersons living routine lives. The central belief of Jains is that all things are imbued with the presence of the life-force, including all living creatures, plants, stones, and all elements, such as air, fire, and water. Other core beliefs include strict adherence to nonviolence, purification of individual karma, commitment to spiritual attainment though continuous rebirth, and vegetarianism. While Jains have several values and practices that are similar to those associated with environmentalism, historically they have focused on otherworldly concerns, such as individual spiritual attainment, rather than on political and social activism.

In Jain cosmology, an individual's position in this incarnation or life is explained by that individual's amount of effort in acting, speaking, and thinking ethically as defined and taught by Jain spiritual leaders, known as Tirthankaras. The Jain position on environmentalism was formally expressed in the 1990 Jain Declaration on Nature (JDN), which was written by L. M. Singhvi when the Jain religion joined the Alliance of Religions and Conservation (ARC). The JDN emphasizes the ecological implications of Jainism, outlines Jain cosmology, describes its codes of conduct, and explains its basic teachings on nonviolence, interdependence, and equanimity. In the JDN, teachings on nonviolence, interdependence, the doctrine of manifold aspects, equanimity, compassion, empathy, and charity are described as the basis of the Jain philosophy of ecological harmony.

The Jain code of conduct requires kindness to animals, vegetarianism, self-restraint and the avoidance of waste, charity, and the five *vratas* (vows). The five *vratas* are considered ethical duties, and consist of intentional nonviolence, seeking and speaking the truth, not stealing or taking by force, practicing restraint and chastity, and practicing nonacquisitiveness. These vows are taken by Jain monks, nuns, and householders or laypersons.

Jainism is associated with environmentally friendly lifestyles but not necessarily environmental activism. Although most Jains restrict religious practices to their personal lives, there have been some Jain nuns, monks, and householders involved in environmental activist campaigns, such as protesting deforestation, advocating for biodiversity, or supporting renewable energy. Similarly, Jain intellectuals have recently asserted that Jainism provides a model for an improved global environmentalism. Because of its focus on the interdependence and interconnectedness of all things, Jainism bears similarity to some aspects of the Gaia hypothesis and the theology of Pierre Teilhard de Chardin, as well as sharing historical and philosophical elements with Hinduism and Buddhism.

See also: Buddhism; Gaia Hypothesis; Hinduism; Teilhard de Chardin, Pierre; Vegetarianism

Further Reading

Rankin, Aidan. 2018. *Jainism and Environmental Philosophy: Karma and the Web of Life*. London: Taylor & Francis.

Judaism

Judaism is a monotheistic religion that originated more than five thousand years ago in the religious culture of the Israelites in the regions known today as Israel and Palestine. It is considered one of the oldest monotheistic religions and is one of the three Abrahamic religious traditions, along with the more recent religions of Christianity and Islam. Around 500 BCE, Judaism emerged as an organized, monotheistic religion with sacred texts, practices, and rituals, and a lineage rooted in the biblical Abraham (ca. 2000–1800 BCE). The Jewish sacred texts are collected in the Tanakh, with the Talmud also being essential to all adherents of Judaism. The Tanakh consists of the Torah, which is the five books of Genesis, Exodus,

Leviticus, Numbers, and Deuteronomy; and the Nevi'im and Ketuvim books of sacred writings. The Talmud, consisting of interpretations of the Torah and rabbinical commentary, provides the foundation for Jewish ethics, customs, laws, and theology.

Contemporary Judaism has three major branches, Orthodox, Conservative, and Reform Judaism, and each has distinct practices and beliefs regarding interpretation of the Rabbinic tradition, interpretation of Jewish law and the Torah, Jewish identity, and numerous other tenets and issues. In 2015 the global Jewish population was estimated at around fifteen million, with a majority of that population located in Israel and the United States. Although there are diverse practices and beliefs in Jewish communities around the world, all are united in the belief in one God, and that the holy word of God, including the Ten Commandments, is written in the Torah.

The various branches of Judaism use many different Torah scriptures and approaches for discovering God's will regarding the relationship between humans and the natural environment. However, all Jewish teaching about the natural environment begins with two scriptures from Genesis in the Torah. In Genesis 1:28, humans are first blessed by God and then told to be "fruitful and multiply and fill the earth and subdue it, and rule over the fish of the sea and over the fowl of the sky and over all the beasts." Genesis 2:15, which states "God took the man . . . and placed him in the Garden of Eden to work it and guard it," is another scripture essential to all Jewish belief about the natural environment.

In general, contemporary Jewish rabbis tend to interpret Genesis 1:28 as a blessing, not as a commandment to dominate the natural world, while Genesis 2:15 is interpreted as God giving humans the responsibility of being guardians and cultivators, not destroyers, of the natural world. There are numerous other Torah laws that restrict human interaction with nature, such as declaring fields should lay fallow for a year, or impose prohibitions against tampering with God's creation by crossbreeding different animal species or cross-grafting tree species. Beyond the essential scriptures from Genesis, Judaism did not have a theology or rabbinical tradition focused on the natural environment until the secular environmental movement emerged in the 1960s.

During the 1960s numerous activists and scholars associated with the secular environmental movement suggested that the Abrahamic religions had been at least partially responsible historically for the exploitation and destruction of nature. Most of these criticisms and the initial responses from Orthodox Jewish scholars occurred in the United States, but over the next few decades, responses came from scholars in all branches of Judaism and from several different countries. In general, Jewish scholars asserted that many of the accusations against Judaism were made by people unfamiliar with Jewish tradition or by non-Jewish scholars who mistranslated or misunderstood Jewish religious texts.

During the 1970s a distinctly Jewish approach to environmental issues began emerging. This approach was developed by Jewish scholars, rabbis, Jewish social justice activists, and others; it incorporated scripture from the Torah and texts from the Talmud; and it suggested how Jewish communities might participate in religiously motivated environmentalism. The first known Jewish environmental organization, Shomrei Adamah, Keepers of the Earth, was founded in 1988 with an emphasis on educating Jewish communities about Jewish environmentalism as well as on publishing related works. Other Jewish environmental organizations were founded in the 1990s, such as the Herschel Center for Environmental Learning and Leadership, located in Israel; the Noah Project, based in the United Kingdom, and the Coalition on the Environment and Jewish Life (COEJL) in Washington, DC.

In the twenty-first century, Judaism has increasingly become involved in sustainability and protecting the natural environment. The three major branches of Orthodox, Conservative, and Reform Judaism have all made formal statements about their commitment to environmentalism and are encouraging Jewish communities and individuals to be socially and politically engaged with environmental issues. Adherents to Orthodox Judaism, the strictest observers of Jewish purity, ethics, and dietary laws, outlined their Torah-based environmental movement in a 2007 statement by the Rabbinical Council of America, making Orthodox involvement relatively recent when compared with other branches of Judaism. Canfei Nesharim, one of the few Orthodox responses so far, is a Torah-based environmental movement organization that is providing opportunities for the Orthodox Jewish community to be socially and politically involved in local, national, and international environmental protection.

Some of Canfei Nesharim's strategies include development and distribution of synagogue programs and educational resources, providing training for Orthodox environmental leaders, and ongoing encouragement for Jewish commitment to environmental action. Recent projects include Teaching Teens Sustainable Living through Jewish Wisdom, weekly distribution of Torah teachings on the environment, and the Uplifting People and Planet project, which published on eighteen environmental topics and created an accompanying study guide in Hebrew and English. Canfei Nesharim, as an Orthodox organization, is committed to Torah-based preservation and protection of the environment and helping "individuals, communities, schools and synagogues internalize Jewish and sustainable values and turn them into an environmentally sensitive way of life."

Conservative Judaism views Jewish law and tradition as shaped by the Jewish people over generations and always developing within historical context. Conservative Judaism avoids strict, unchanging theological definitions and believes Judaism is defined not only by traditional sources and the Torah but also by its living adherents, historical context, and critical analysis of contemporary issues. Conservative Judaism has a history of involvement in environmentalism dating back at least to the 1970s. The Women's League for Conservative Judaism (WLCJ) is representative of the numerous organizations that have been defining Jewish environmentalism since the 1970s. It is a primarily a national organization serving communities in the United States but also has several ongoing international projects.

WLCJ has published several resolutions on environmental issues since 1978, asserting that the environment "has certain unalienable rights, and these rights are endowed to it by the Creator" and that the "Bible mandates us to tend God's garden; that the world is a precious gift that has been entrusted to humanity. Therefore, it is our obligation, to ensure that nothing we do diminishes any of God's creations." Similarly, the Rabbinical Assembly, the international association of Conservative rabbis, has passed several resolutions since 1990 that request Conservative Jewish members to take action on environmental issues such as climate change, hydraulic fracturing, environmental concerns in Israel, endangered species, banning of nuclear testing, and sustainable energy. Both WLJC and the Rabbinical Assembly publish guidelines to help individuals and communities implement lifestyles that are environmentally sustainable and based in Conservative Judaism.

Reform Judaism, the most socially and politically progressive of the three major branches, values ethics over ceremony and ritual and teaches that each individual Jew must decide whether or not, and to what extent, to follow Jewish traditional laws. It does not insist on a unified theological canon, and its membership policy emphasizes acceptance and inclusivity, with open invitations to all people to join or participate in its communities. The Religious Action Center of Reform Judaism (RAC) is most representative of Jewish environmentalism in the twenty-first century, and although focused on U.S. political action, it has international networks and global projects, and it builds alliances among the different branches of Judaism. RAC has been active in U.S. social justice work since 1961 and "mobilizes around federal, state, and local legislation; supports and develops congregational leaders; and organizes communities to create a world overflowing with justice, compassion, and peace." RAC is involved in numerous ongoing environmentalist efforts that include opposition to drilling in the Arctic National Wildlife Refuge, networking with the Kibbutz Lotan Eco-Jewish Community in Israel, protecting endangered species, and participation in the environmental justice movement.

Recent RAC initiatives, in collaboration with several branches of Judaism and other religions, provide examples of how Judaism is increasingly shaping environmental policies that have national and global implications. RAC's 2017 Resolution on Addressing the Impacts of Climate Change encourages congregations to take political action, to advocate for governments to "uphold or go beyond the commitments of the Paris Climate Agreement," to educate and prepare for the impacts of climate change, to advocate for "legislative, regulatory, and judicial action" on climate change, and to push the Canadian and U.S. governments to uphold their international responsibilities related to climate change, and to continue building interreligious networks. RAC's 2019 resolution urging support for the Green New Deal is another recent initiative representative of its religiously motivated environmental activism. RAC supports the Green New Deal as exemplifying the Jewish concept of the *shmita* year, in which the land is allowed to rest. RAC's legislative representative for 2019 explained that the transition "to a 100 percent clean and renewable energy economy is the ultimate shmita, protecting the Earth and all its inhabitants from the devastating impacts of climate change. This commitment to environmental protection and conservation also exists from the very moment God put humans on Earth."

See also: Climate Change; Environmental Justice; Hydraulic Fracturing; Religious Environmental Movement

Further Reading

Benstein, Jeremy. 2006. *The Way into Judaism and the Environment.* Woodstock, VT: Jewish Lights Pub.

Yoreh, Tanhum. 2019. *Waste Not: A Jewish Environmental Ethic.* Albany: State University of New York Press.

L

Laudato Si'

Laudato Si': On Care for Our Common Home is a 184-page encyclical published by Pope Francis I, of the Roman Catholic Church, in June 2015. The encyclical's title, *Laudato Si'* (medieval central Italian for "praise be"), comes from the *Canticle of the Sun*, a thirteenth-century poem by Saint Francis of Assisi that praises God for creating all the creatures and things in the universe. In the 2015 encyclical, Pope Francis explains that environmental degradation and global warming, among other problems, are the consequence of consumerism and irresponsible development. He asserts that unified, immediate action is required to address and solve these problems, and that human stewardship of the natural world is an essential element of the church's teaching on social justice. Encyclicals are the Catholic Church's formal teaching documents directed at all Catholics, and *Laudato Si'* is the first encyclical in the history of the church to address the relationship between humans and the natural environment.

Pope Francis's stated intention in *Laudato Si'* is to encourage discussion about what he sees as the developed world's unbridled pursuit of economic gains and indifference to the destruction of the planet. He argues that human behaviors and social attitudes have led to an environmental crisis and "disposable culture" in which unwanted items and people, such as the elderly and poor, are treated as waste or trash. The encyclical includes critical discussions of environmental problems, such as pollution and climate change, and their perceived core causes, including unrestrained economic growth and market capitalism. Francis also calls for an "integral ecology" that expands Catholic social teaching and emphasizes justice as part of a "global ecological conversion" necessary for the common good of the planet and all people. As part of this global ecological conversion, Francis urges interreligious and interdisciplinary cooperation and dialogue that includes the political, economic, religious, and scientific aspects of environmental problems. All individuals, nations, and Christian communities, he asserts, must take seriously "ecological education" so they can learn new "lifestyles" that embrace the "covenant between humanity and the environment."

In *Laudato Si'*, Francis also provides an extensive examination of the theological and biblical underpinnings of his assertions and solutions. He discusses the historical problem in the Judeo-Christian tradition regarding the concept of "dominion" and suggests that this concept must be replaced with an emphasis on the interconnectedness of all things. He asserts that immediate action is needed and notes it "must be said that some committed and prayerful Christians, with the excuse of realism and pragmatism, tend to ridicule expressions of concern for the environment. Others are passive; they choose not to change their habits and thus become inconsistent." He clearly states that these Christians who fail to act need "an 'ecological conversion,' whereby the effects of their encounter with Jesus Christ become evident in their relationship with the world around them."

See also: Francis of Assisi; Pope Francis I

Further Reading

Francis, Pope. 2015. *Praise Be to You: Laudato Si': On Care for Our Common Home*. San Francisco: Ignatius Press.

M

Marine Conservation

Marine conservation, a subdiscipline of conservation biology, refers to the study, preservation, and protection of marine ecosystems and their plant and animal species. Also known as ocean conservation and marine resources conservation, the field of marine conservation emerged in the 1970s globally as a response to challenges such as extinction and loss of biodiversity, habitat degradation, and anthropogenic damage to marine ecosystems. Some of the current issues in marine conservation include marine debris and microplastics, dying coral reefs, oil spills and chemical contamination, ocean acidification, and climate change issues such as warmer ocean temperatures and sea level rise. Numerous issues, such as whaling, protecting breeding and feeding areas for marine species, managing invasive species, shark finning, and unsustainable fishing practices globally are directly related to biodiversity and environmental sustainability. Marine conservation scientists study both the global marine ecosystem and its many interdependent smaller ecosystems, as well as their interdependence with all of Earth's various ecosystems. The field of marine conservation relies on several sciences, including marine biology and oceanography, and the expertise of other areas, such as economics; policy making at the local, regional, national, and global levels; and marine law. Strategies used to address marine conservation issues include creating and enforcing laws, establishing protected habitats, studying the populations and migrations of marine species, and changing human behaviors that have negative impacts on marine ecosystems. Although it is difficult to change human behaviors, this is a crucial strategy that involves understanding the cultures of communities and their interdependence with marine ecosystems.

Religion and spirituality are essential elements of most communities and shape the way its members interact with the natural environment, including marine ecosystems. Although religious beliefs and practices were not initially included in marine conservation projects and studies, recently marine conservationists have recognized that spiritually and religiously motivated groups, including Indigenous communities, are an important source of support and information. The Religion and Conservation Biology Working Group of the Society for Conservation Biology (RCBWG) is an example of marine conservationists' recognition of religious groups as important collaborators. At the 2016 International Marine Conservation Congress (IMCC), the RCBWG held information sessions and an open forum on why religious communities and groups are important to marine conservation, and how to develop constructive interaction with them.

As part of the RCBWG's activities and events at the 2016 IMCC, participants shared their experiences and research about behaviors and attitudes that might interfere or deter relationships with religious or faith communities. These discussions led to the creation and initiation of the RCBWG *Best Practices Guidelines for Interacting with Faith-based Leaders and Communities*, which recommends that ethics, cultural values, and spiritual and religious worldviews be considered in marine conservation initiatives and conservation science in general. At the next International Marine Conservation Congress in 2018, focus groups shared their experiences related to implementation of the *Best Practices Guidelines*, as well as their quantitative and qualitative assessments of these relatively new guidelines. Although the formal study of religious practices and beliefs is a relatively recent development in the marine conservation sciences, many communities and organizations have been practicing religiously and spiritually motivated marine conservation for several decades or even generations.

Examples of marine conservation rooted in religious or spiritual beliefs include Interfaith Oceans, A Rocha Kenya (ARK), and numerous Malaysian Buddhists and Muslims involved in conservation of the Western Malaysian leatherback turtle and its marine ecosystem. Interfaith Oceans, founded in 2012, has members from Buddhist, Christian, Islamic, Jewish, and Indigenous traditions that facilitate "collaborations between different religions and spiritual paths with ocean science and conservation to preserve and restore the oceans and their wild and human communities." Interfaith Oceans' global initiatives include sustainable fisheries, marine sanctuaries, plastic reduction, and ocean restoration and protection. ARK, another example of religiously motivated marine conservation, is an inter-denominational Christian organization registered since 1999 as a nongov-ernmental, environmental organization. Located near the Indian Ocean, ARK's marine conservation projects include the Hawkfish Ecology Project, which sponsors research on coral reefs in Watamu Marine National Park and the Tana River Delta Conservation Project. Protection of the Malaysian leatherback sea turtle is another example of religiously moti-vated marine conservation. Buddhist and Muslim leaders in Malaysia have assisted marine conservationists by creating public interest in protecting the turtles, performing science-informed Buddhist turtle rituals, and con-necting marine species conservation with Islamic beliefs about environ-mental stewardship.

See also: Biodiversity; Sustainability

Further Reading

Moyer, Joanne. 2015. "Faith-Based Sustainability in Practice: Case Studies from Kenya." *Journal for the Study of Religion, Nature and Culture* 9 (1): 42–67.

Northcott, Michael. 2012. "Buddhist Rituals, Mosque Sermons, and Marine Turtles: Religion, Ecology, and the Conservation of a Dinosaur in West Malaysia." *Journal for the Study of Religion, Nature & Culture* 6 (2): 196–214.

Sodhi, Navjot S., and Paul R. Ehrlich. 2011. *Conservation Biology for All.* Oxford: Oxford University Press.

N

National Religious Partnership for the Environment

The National Religious Partnership for the Environment (NRPE) is a U.S. interreligious collaboration among the U. S. Conference of Catholic Bishops, the National Council of Churches, the Coalition of Jewish Communities and Environment, and the Evangelical Environmental Network (EEN). Since its inception in 1993, NRPE has funded numerous programs that address environmental issues through its membership, made up of more than 114 million individuals and 156,000 U.S. religious congregations. NRPE's research mission is to encourage scholarship on religious environmentalism and to disseminate this knowledge to religious communities. NRPE's spiritual mission is "encourage people of faith to weave values and programs of care for God's creation throughout the entire fabric of religious life" through liturgy, theological study, Earth stewardship, social ministry, and engagement with policy makers.

Through dissemination of research, political strategy, and investigation of environmental policies, NRPE has led U.S. religious leaders and communities in numerous political efforts over the years. NRPE coordinated the efforts of evangelical leaders in signing the 1993 Evangelical Environmental Declaration. Similarly, NRPE worked with prominent scientists and religious leaders to create the 2004 document "Earth's Climate Embraces Us All: A Plea from Religion and Science for Action on Global Climate Change," which requested that U.S. Congress take immediate action on proposed climate change legislation. Other NRPE advocacy campaigns have addressed energy use, deforestation, biodiversity, and children's environmental health. NRPE has also provided workshops on environmental issues, including strategies to increase media coverage, for religious leaders, labor unions, secular environmental organizations, and corporations.

NRPE currently focuses on issues related to climate, species protection, water, and land as well as climate-related issues such as clean power, international climate negotiations, and clean cars. Additionally, NRPE campaigns in support of the U.S. Endangered Species Act (ESA), and asserts that the United States should be working to strengthen the ESA, known as the "Noah's Ark of conservation laws" by religious environmentalists. On water issues, NRPE worked to prevent the EPA from reversing the 2015 Clean Water Rule and has continuously requested religious individuals and communities to submit formal, written prayers to the EPA as part of the 1,000 Prayers for Clean Water campaign. Regarding land-related issues, NRPE's recent work focuses on offshore drilling, national parks, and public lands. NPRE has publicly opposed "expanded oil and gas drilling, as well as seismic testing, in public waters" and states that "offshore drilling brings unacceptable risks to God's oceans and coastal communities." NPRE had actively opposed both drilling in the U.S. Arctic Wildlife Refuge and the reduction of national monuments, such as Bears Ears and Grand Staircase-Escalante. NPRE describes all its campaigns and projects as essential to being "good caretakers of God's creation."

See also: Climate Change; Evangelical Environmental Network; Water

Further Reading

National Religious Partnership for the Environment. 1995. *Models of Engagement: Environmentally Active Congregations*. New York: National Religious Partnership for the Environment.

Nature Religions

Nature religion refers to a broad category of religious and spiritual traditions that are based in a reverence for nature, a belief in the interconnectedness of all things in the natural world, and the symbolic and literal inclusion of nature in ritual and practice. By the 1970s adherents, researchers, and scholars were increasingly using the term formally to describe belief systems that are nature-centered, including folk religions, Paganism, deep radical ecology, Indigenous spirituality, Gaian spirituality, and ecofeminism. Followers of nature religions often view their beliefs and practices as emerging from the remnants of much older spiritualities, philosophies, or theologies that were repressed over the centuries by dominant or colonizing religious institutions. Additionally, nature religions are seen as favoring decentralized political and social authority, resisting exploitative globalization, and encouraging spiritual enlightenment through nature. Subcultures based on outdoor activities, such as surfing, that involve a nature-based spiritually and spiritual language to describe the activity, have also been identified by some scholars as nature religions.

Beginning in the 1970s, religious studies scholar Catherine Albanese provided a general description of nature religion as a diverse range of beliefs and practices that use nature as their primary symbolic resource. She also asserted that religions "are action systems as much, if not more than, they are thought systems" and in her research over the years has provided examples of nature religion as a motivation for political thought and action. In her many books and articles, Albanese has noted several different types of spiritualities, theologies, and philosophies as examples of nature religion, including those of Amerindians and U.S. historical figures such as Thomas Jefferson, Ralph Waldo Emerson, Henry David Thoreau, and John Muir. She provides historical evidence that the nature-centered thought and ideas of these individuals and groups influenced different cultural, political, and social movements throughout U.S. history. Albanese focuses almost exclusively on nature religion as a persistent force in North America, but many other scholars have used her work as a springboard to study nature religions in diverse forms around the world.

In the twenty-first century, the term *nature religion* has been used to describe earth-based spirituality in the U.S. Pacific-Northwest, Shinto in Japan, various Indigenous beliefs, radical environmentalism, feminist witchcraft, ecofeminism, whitewater kayaking subcultures, and numerous other distinct spiritual, religious, and philosophical subcultures or belief systems. Bron Taylor, a U.S. conservationist and professor of religion and nature, has written extensively for several decades on nature religion and related topics. In his research on nature religion, he has noted the extreme diversity among its adherents, which includes "pagans, scientists, environmentalists, as well as social scientists and religion scholars, and participants in international institutions and nongovernmental groups who are engaged in dialog and action related to the quest for environmental sustainability." According to Taylor, these various individuals and groups share two basic characteristics: (1) "A perception that nature is sacred and worthy of care"; and (2) "Feelings of belonging and connection to the earth---of being bound to and dependent upon earth's living systems."

Scholars have offered increasingly diverse perspectives regarding the impact of nature religion on political behavior. Several historical studies have documented a connection between nature religions and racist sub-cultures and political movements in Europe, such as historian Anna Bramwell's research noting the fusion of nature religion with Nazism and eugenics programs. Other scholars, such as geographer Clarence Glacken, have asserted that nature religions are beneficent, both spiritually and eco-logically, and continue to provide wisdom useful in understanding human interaction with the natural environment. Similarly, ethnographical studies of contemporary Paganism have documented that the beliefs associated with nature religions provide committed, persistent motivation for envi-ronmental activism in Pagan individuals and their communities. Recently, researchers and environmentalists have also used the term *nature religion* to denote emerging syncretic religious perspectives, such as those of activ-ists in the U.S. Appalachia region who forcefully resist mountain-top removal coal mining and other environmentally degrading practices.

See also: Ecofeminism; Folk Religions; Gaia Hypothesis; Paganism; Shinto

Further Reading

Albanese, Catherine L. 1991. *Nature Religion in America: From the Algonkian Indians to the New Age.* Chicago: University of Chicago Press.

Taylor, Bron Raymond. 2010. *Dark Green Religion: Nature Spirituality and the Planetary Future.* Berkeley: University of California Press.

Witt, Joseph D. 2016. *Religion and Resistance in Appalachia: Faith and the Fight Against Mountaintop Removal Coal Mining.* Lexington: University Press of Kentucky.

New Age Movement

The *New Age movement* refers to a cultural shift in religious practices and spirituality that became apparent to the general public in the late 1960s, mostly in the United Kingdom and North America. It is usually seen as a synthesis of Western esoteric paths—such as Theosophy—Eastern religious mysticism, and other practices and beliefs used to assist individuals in discovering their inner divine nature and participating in spiritual evolution. The term *New Age* appeared as early as 1944 in the theosophical writings of Alice Bailey, which were a synthesis of ideas and beliefs from several different religious traditions, mysticism, astrology, and psychology. By early 1970s, the term was used to refer to a diverse range of belief systems and practices, such as channeling, card reading, meditation, astrology, homoeopathy, ley lines, Reiki, and yoga, that focus on the potential of finding enlightenment or healing in the individual self. In New Age thought, if individuals are able to discover inner divinity or potential, then they will be able to more effectively participate in external political and social transformation.

A general premise in most New Age belief systems is that a coming global crisis can be prevented if enough people experience individual enlightenment and personal transformation. In New Age thought, there is often an association with the Age of Aquarius, when planetary alignments, along with other astronomical phenomena, are interpreted by astrologers as ushering in a time marked by the expansion of human consciousness and humanitarian tendencies. Additionally, environmentalist themes, such saving the planet from destruction and an interrelatedness with the natural world, are common interests found across the diverse organizations and spiritual paths associated with the New Age movement. Some characteristics of the New Age movement, such as mysticism and nature religions, predate the emergence of the secular environmental movement, while other characteristics appeared later, such as the incorporation of the Gaia hypothesis and the theology of Pierre Teilhard de Chardin.

Although New Agers typically focus first on individual enlightenment, most share a concern for the environment that is both political and connected to their spirituality. It is difficult to define New Age beliefs as predominantly either politically left or right. The New Age movement shares some position with the political left, including support of alternative sexuality and nontraditional options to marriage, population control, global unity, rejection of male dominance, and globally regulated environmental policies. However, the movement also shares views with the political right, such as rejection of extensive national government bureaucracies, a preference for local political authority and autonomy, individualism and self-reliance, and unimpeded personal freedom. In the New Age movement, political engagement is often grounded in beliefs in a planetary consciousness, the sacredness of nature, the oneness of all humanity, and the interdependence of all life and of nation-states.

See also: Gaia Hypothesis; Nature Religions; Paganism; Teilhard de Chardin, Pierre

Further Reading

Campion, Nicholas. 2016. *The New Age in the Modern West: Counterculture, Utopia and Prophecy from the Late Eighteenth Century to the Present Day.* New York: Bloomsbury.

Satin, Mark Ivor. 1979. *New Age Politics: Healing Self and Society.* New York: Dell.

O

Overpopulation

Human overpopulation occurs when there are more people than can be sustained by habitat, biome, ecosystem, or environment. If a population's number is too high to be continuously sustained by available resources, such as clean water, clean air, and food, then that population has exceeded the carrying capacity of its habitat or environment, and the lives of future generations are jeopardized. Overpopulation, which can refer to a specific regional population or to the world's population, can ultimately result in ecological collapses and irreparable damage to a habitat, ecosystem, or planet. Some of the effects of human overpopulation include pollution, loss of biodiversity, increased unemployment, increased cost of living, and increases in conflicts and wars. Causes of overpopulation include increases in birth rates, declines in mortality rates, and improved nutrition and health care that increase survival rates and life expectancy. As of 2019 the planet's human population is more than 7.7 billion. Estimates of Earth's carrying capacity range from 4 billion to 16 billion, with the population expected to reach 10 billion by 2050. Scientists, demographers, and policy makers are considering strategies for avoiding overpopulation, including increased education, family planning, benefits or concessions for families having fewer children, and technologies that will ensure resources are replenished.

Historically, reproduction and family size have often been the focus of discussions about the connections between religion and overpopulation. The Abrahamic religions, which include Judaism, Christianity, and Islam, all have branches that actively encourage human reproduction within families made up of married individuals and their children. In Judaism, practices related to reproduction and birth control vary, with Orthodox Judaism being the least accepting of birth control, and the ultra-Orthodox Haredi group having the highest birth rate. In Christianity, there are several branches that have relatively high birth rates and prioritize large families in their teachings, including the Amish, Apostolic Lutherans in Finland and Sweden, the Quiverfull movement in conservative Protestantism, the Church of Jesus Christ of Latter-day Saints, and Catholics in some regions of the world.

In some Christian branches and groups, there is a rejection of birth control and an emphasis on God's instructions in Genesis 1:28 to "be fruitful, and multiply." In Islam, procreation is encouraged in the Hadith scriptures, but the Qur'an has no clear teaching on birth control and most Islamic traditions permit birth control and family planning. In Hinduism there is an emphasis on sustainability, and many adherents believe that producing more children than they can support goes against the principle of ahimsa (nonviolence). In India, where around 80 percent of the population, or more than one million people, are adherents of Hinduism, overpopulation is considered an environmental and economic issue, and Indians overall do not see birth control as an ethical or religious issue. Most Buddhists believe it is unethical to kill sentient creatures, with some viewing fertilized eggs as already sentient. However, a majority of Buddhists believe that birth control that prevents fertilization is acceptable and ethical.

Beliefs and practices related to reproduction and family size vary within and among religious traditions. Additionally, regional differences of economics, culture, education, and other variables have an impact on religious beliefs and practices related to reproduction. However, in terms of world averages, major world religions and their adherents do not have higher fertility rates that would cause overpopulation globally. Data sets collected from 2010 to 2015 by the Pew Research Center show the world's overall fertility rate at 2.5 children per woman, which is slightly above the statistical replacement level of 2. On a scale from lowest to highest, global fertility rates are as follows: Buddhists, 1.6; "other" religions, 1.7; folk religions, 1.8; Jews, 2.3; Hindus, 2.4; world overall, 2.5; Christians, 2.7; and Muslims, 3.1.

Of the major religions, Christians and Muslims are the only categories above the world's overall average fertility rate of 2.5, with the fertility of Hindus and Jews falling below the world average and Buddhists having the lowest fertility rate of all. However, when religious beliefs about reproduction contribute to higher birth rates in impoverished regions with few resources, then religion becomes a contributing factor to overpopulation.

Scientific population predictions for 2050 show that all major religious traditions are expected to increase their population numbers, with the exception of Buddhism. In the upcoming decades, even though there will be numerical growth in religious populations, overall these populations will not grow at the same rate as the total global population and so will constitute a slightly smaller percentage of the population by 2050. Currently, the world's average fertility rates indicate that religions in general do not contribute to overpopulation of the world more than most other groups, although there are regional instances of overpopulation driven by a number of factors that include religious beliefs.

See also: Biodiversity; Folk Religions; Food Security; Pollution; Sustainability

Further Reading

Kaufmann, Eric P. 2010. *Shall the Religious Inherit the Earth? Demography and Politics in the Twenty-First Century.* London: Profile Books.

Pew Research Center. 2015. *The Future of World Religions: Population Growth: Projections, 2010–2050.* Washington, DC: Pew Research Center.

Tal, Alon. 2017. *The Land Is Full: Addressing Overpopulation in Israel.* New Haven, CT: Yale University Press.

United Nations Department for Economic and Social Affairs. 2019. *World Population Prospects 2019: Highlights.* New York: Author.

P

Paganism

Contemporary Paganism, sometimes referred to as modern Paganism or Neo-Paganism, includes a wide range of belief systems that are usually described as a type of nature-centered spirituality or religion. The term *pagan* comes from the Latin word *paganus*, which was initially used by early Christians in reference to non-Christians, and later used as a label for people from rural areas. Contemporary Paganism is often considered by historians as a revivalist or reconstructed tradition, but Pagans themselves usually trace its origins to the ancient practices and beliefs of their spiritual or physical ancestors. Celtic Paganism, Wicca, Goddess-Feminist, Druid, Hellenism, Rodnovery, Romuva, and Asatru are some of the prominent collective identities in twenty-first-century Paganism, although there are numerous others around the world. Because these identities are seen by some scholars as modern reconstructions or recent revivals, they are sometimes referred to as new religious movements. Commonly held beliefs or themes among contemporary Paganisms include animism, polytheism, pantheism, the power and sacredness of nature, and the interconnectedness of all things. Because of their spiritual and religious focus on nature, many Pagans are involved in environmental activism or consider themselves to be environmentalists.

Many distinct groups and traditions within Paganism share enough general beliefs and practices that they willingly celebrate or participate together in public rituals and festivals. Because most of its adherents believe nature is sacred and supremely powerful, with all its elements interconnected, Paganism is often described as both a type of animism and a nature religion. As such, private and public rituals and celebrations occur at times synchronized with the natural world, such as seasonal changes or planetary and celestial events. Most Pagan traditions celebrate the summer and winter solstices, spring and vernal equinoxes, and the seasonal midpoints between these celestial events. Eclipses and lunar phases also have spiritual or religious significance, and along with solstices, equinoxes, and seasonal midpoints, are seen as sacred natural events ideal for divination or rituals that celebrate transitions in life, such as stages in an initiatory path, birth of children, puberty, or handfasting and other types of marriage. Additionally, some groups, such as Icelandic and Slavic Pagan traditions, are tied to a specific land, region, and ethnic ancestry and are defined as folk religions by some contemporary scholars and adherents. Other Pagan belief systems, such as the Wiccan and Druid traditions, are typically not focused on ethnicity or tribal ancestry and have a much larger global membership.

Although based on elements of pre-Christian Indigenous religion and folk practices, contemporary Wicca had its first followers in the 1940s. Wicca was promoted across the United Kingdom by several occultists such as Gerald Gardner and Doreen Valiente in the 1940s and 1950s, and by the 1960s it had gained followers in the United States. By the 1970s variations of Wicca influenced by local and regional cultures were emerging across Europe, the Americas, South Africa, New Zealand, Australia, and more recently in other developed countries such as Japan. Wicca tends to be organized into small groups of friends that conduct seasonal rituals and ceremonies together, sometimes called covens, with members avoiding proselytizing or advocating Wiccan beliefs in public settings.

Wicca beliefs and rituals vary widely among groups, but most Wiccans emphasize the importance of mystery and magic, commitment to personal transformation, acknowledgment of both feminine and masculine powers or deities, and above all the sacredness and interconnectedness of all things in nature. Although there are no formally recognized sacred texts in Wicca, almost all Wiccans follow both the Wiccan Rede, best known by its final line—"do what you will, so long as it harms none"—and the "law of threefold effect," by which the effects of a person's actions are increased three times in power and returned to the person.

The contemporary Druid tradition is a type of nature religion or nature-centered spirituality that originated in the Druid Revival of the 1700s in the United Kingdom. Most Druids trace their spiritual roots back to ancient Indo-European folk practices. There are several formal Druid orders, with some having distinctly international membership and others being better defined as folk religions that emphasize local or regional membership. When compared with Wiccans, contemporary Druid groups tend to be much larger in size, are usually referred to as groves, and more frequently practice their rituals outdoors in public areas, such as in large meadows, parks, groves, or forests.

Each Druid order has its own tradition and organizational structure. Examples of variation in status and organizational structure include the nonprofit-religion status of the UK Druid Network; Ár nDraíocht Féin (ADF) registered as a church in the United States; and the initiatory pathway model of the Order of Bards, Ovates, and Druids (OBOD), which has an international membership and welcomes the integration of other religious traditions into Druidry. All Druid organizations place great significance on stone monuments, such as Stonehenge in Wiltshire, United Kingdom, botanical knowledge and tree lore, celestial events and star lore, and connecting with spiritual ancestors or ancestors in a family lineage. Druid orders have formal structure, and there is cooperation among the different orders, which has contributed to many Druids being involved in organized environmental activism.

All Pagans have a spirituality centered in nature and are committed to protecting the natural environment, with some using private ritual and meditation, some practicing large group rituals in public, and others involved in direct action radical environmental protests. Pagan environmentalist efforts have included different issues and strategies, such as protesting construction and development that destroys forests or wildlife habitat, antifracking protests, and protecting natural areas surrounding culturally important sites. The EcoPagan Network is an example of the increase in organized environmentalism motivated by Pagan beliefs in the twenty-first century. EcoPagan is an international network that uses digital technology and social networking to disseminate information to Pagans, mobilize Pagan action around environmental issues, promote environmentalism in Pagan ritual, and encourage interreligious cooperation on environmental issues.

See also: Animism; Folk Religions; Nature Religions

Further Reading

Byghan, Yowann. 2018. *Modern Druidism: An Introduction.* Jefferson, NC: McFarland & Company.

Harvey, Graham. 2011. *Contemporary Paganism: Religions of the Earth from Druids and Witches to Heathens and Ecofeminists.* New York: New York University Press.

White, Ethan. 2015. *Wicca: History, Belief, and Community in Modern Pagan Witchcraft.* New York: Sussex Academic Press.

Paris Agreement

The Paris Agreement is an international agreement on climate change that was negotiated and drafted by 196 countries in 2015 and approved by the United Nations in 2016. The Paris Agreement, also referred to as the Paris Agreement on Climate Change, was created under the auspices of the United Nations Framework Convention on Climate Change (UNFCCC). As an international agreement, it is focused on the reduction of greenhouse gas emissions globally and the development of strategies for mitigating, adapting, and financing that reduction globally. Its main goal is to limit the global average temperature increase to 2 degrees Celsius (3.6 degrees Fahrenheit) above preindustrial levels, with each country developing its own plan for contributing to the mitigation of global warming. Limiting the global temperature increase will reduce the effects and risks associated with climate change. Countries are expected to review their plans regularly and adjust their actions accordingly, to meet 2030 emissions targets related to limiting the global average temperature increase. By March 2019, the Paris Agreement had been signed by 195 UNFCCC member countries and ratified by 185. Religious leaders and institutions from around the world have formally supported the Paris Agreement, criticized leaders or countries that reject it, and independently monitored environmental policies for compliance.

Religious traditions and their leaders have supported the Paris Agreement, participated in the dissemination of information on climate change, and created plans of action that will contribute to the reduction of emissions. Religious leaders submitted the Interfaith Climate Change Statement to World Leaders to the UN in March 2016 in support of the Paris Agreement, asserting that "we must begin a transition away from polluting fossil fuels and toward clean energy sources" and "strive for alternatives to the culture of consumerism that is so destructive to ourselves and to our planet." In this statement, religious leaders made several formal requests, including the ratification and implementation of the Paris Agreement by all countries; an increase in the flow of funds to support reduction; rapid divestment of all fossil fuel subsidies; transition from fossil fuels to renewable energy by 2050; and full commitment by faith communities to reduce emissions in all areas of their lives. The formal statement also provides theological, spiritual, and ethical reasons for supporting the Paris Agreement and notes that "climate change presents our global family with the opportunity to embark on a path of spiritual renewal defined by greater ecological awareness and action."

Several interreligious organizations have been very active in support of the Paris Agreement. The Parliament of the World's Religions, through its Climate Action Task Force, worked with government leaders, universities, and businesses to create the We Are Still In campaign, in which participants pledged their continued support for, and expressed concern at U.S. withdrawal in 2017 from, the Paris Agreement. Another organization, Interfaith Power and Light (IPL), maintains a publicly accessible online archive of religious statements on both climate change and the Paris Agreement.

See also: Climate Change; Interfaith Power and Light

Further Reading

Klein, Daniel R., María Pía Carazo, Meinhard Doelle, Jane Bulmer, and Andrew Higham, eds. 2017. *The Paris Agreement on Climate Change: Analysis and Commentary.* Oxford: Oxford University Press.

Pollution

Pollution, in the context of resource management and environmentalism, refers to introduction of contaminants into the air, land, and water that are harmful to animals, plants, and ecosystems. Types of pollution include air pollution, soil contamination, land pollution, and water pollution and are found in rural, agricultural, wilderness, and urban environments. Some types of pollution, such as electromagnetic, noise, light, and radioactive contamination tend to be clustered in and around urban environments or industrial sites. All types of pollution have measurable negative impacts on ecosystems and their life-forms. Since the 1800s, both urbanization and industrialization have expanded globally, resulting in significant increases in pollution and related environmental health risks. The World Health Organization (WHO) estimates that more than twelve million people die annually from environmental health risks caused by pollution, with most of those people living in developing or low-income countries. Globally, pollution control policies target several areas of human activity, including overconsumption, agriculture, manufacturing, extraction and mining, transportation, and the lifestyles of individuals and communities. Pollution control strategies implemented by governments and other organizations include reduction of carbon emissions, reduction of plastic products and microplastics, capture and treatment of waste and contaminants, elimination of pesticides and herbicides from agriculture, and promotion of environmental sustainability.

Overall, in the twenty-first century, religious traditions and their adherents do not intentionally contribute to pollution problems. They are more likely to be involved in controlling pollution through environmentally sustainable practices, political participation, or traditional ecological knowledge (TEK). There are exceptions, such as the Holi festival in India that results in substantial air pollution and water pollution at the end of every winter, but interreligious cooperation aimed at controlling pollution is more common. Examples of the many interreligious collaborations on pollution issues include religious leaders in the United States requesting stronger regulations on carbon emissions and religious leaders fighting air pollution in Jakarta, the capital city of Indonesia.

Concerned that the U.S. Environmental Protection Agency would weaken the 1970 Clean Air Act, leaders from the Baha'i, Buddhist, Jewish, Hindu, and Christian traditions and representatives from Interfaith Power and Light (IPL) and World Council of Churches (WCC) all testified at an EPA hearing in 2014. These leaders and organizations argued specifically for increased regulation of carbon emissions generated by coal plants in the United States and have continued to be politically involved in pollution issues in the years since. Another example of interreligious collaboration on air pollution occurred in 2019, when religious leaders from several religious traditions, including Buddhism, Christianity, Confucianism, Hinduism, and Islam, agreed to take active roles in reducing carbon emissions in Jakarta. Working with local government agencies, these religious leaders continue to be instrumental in encouraging the population to reduce pollution, including a 30 percent reduction in Jakarta's carbon emissions by 2030.

Religions are also involved in controlling pollution through formal statements made by religious authorities and leaders who are responsible for representing their religious tradition's position on issues. A few of the many recent examples include statements and initiatives on pollution from the Catholic Church's Pope Francis I, the Orthodox Church's Patriarch Bartholomew I of Constantinople, and Indonesia's Muslim religious leaders. On the 2018 annual World Day of Prayer for the Care of Creation, Pope Francis released an official pontifical message urging Christians to address water pollution, declaring that society "cannot allow our seas and oceans to be littered by endless fields of floating plastic." Patriarch Bartholomew also made statements on pollution in 2018, asserting that the "atmosphere is being polluted more and more with each passing day; clean water is becoming scarcer since we are polluting our oceans, rivers and lakes."

In 2019 leaders from Indonesia's largest Islamic organizations Nahdlatul Ulama (NU) and Muhammadiyah began a partnership with the Indonesian government aimed at reducing plastic pollution. Indonesia is one of the world's major plastic polluters and is estimated to be the source of 10 percent of the world's plastic waste. Muslim leaders from these organizations made a commitment to change the behaviors of an estimated one hundred million Indonesian Muslims, with an emphasis on reducing the use of disposable plastics, including shopping bags, food containers, eating utensils, and other plastics that pollute air, land, and water. NU and Muhammadiyah released a joint statement declaring that they will be "carrying out a plastic bag use reduction movement, which is part of an Islamic culture, by implementing it in numerous activities from childhood to adult level."

In addition to interreligious initiatives and formal position statements made by prominent religious leaders, religious communities around the world fight pollution locally and regionally, motivated by their religious beliefs and values. For example, Buddhist monastic groups in the Sisaket province of northeastern Thailand developed a plan for a temple complex built out of the recyclable objects and materials they were collecting. These monastic groups were deeply concerned about the illegally dumped toxic waste, the 2,500 open landfills, and the excessive consumer use of plastics that contribute to Thailand's pollution crisis, which spills over into the planet's oceans. In 1984 the Buddhist monks began construction of the Wat Pa Maha Kaew temple complex, which is constructed primarily of beer bottles, and opened the temple to the public in 1986. Communities and governments in the region also joined in the recycling efforts, contributing beer bottles and other waste materials to the temple construction project. Wat Pa Maha Kaew, also known as the Temple of a Million Bottles, has more than twenty buildings constructed of more than 1.5 million bottles with mosaics created from bottle caps. The Buddhist monks view their commitment to sustainability and recycling as an expression of their religious beliefs and values. The monks also believe that their efforts encourage Thailand's population to address pollution problems and practice environmental sustainability.

See also: Bartholomew I of Constantinople; Climate Change; Interfaith Power and Light; Marine Conservation; Pope Francis I; World Council of Churches

Further Reading

Gade, Anna M. 2015. "Islamic Law and the Environment in Indonesia." *Worldviews: Global Religions, Culture & Ecology* 19 (2): 161–83.

Mohamad, Zeeda, Noorshahzila Idris, and Zuffri Mamat. 2012. "Role of Religious Communities in Enhancing Transition Experiments: A Localised Strategy for Sustainable Solid Waste Management in Malaysia." *Sustainability Science* 7 (2): 237–51.

Pachauri, Tripti, Vyoma Singla, Aparna Satsangi, Anita Lakhani, and K. Kumari. 2013. "Characterization of Major Pollution Events (Dust, Haze, and Two Festival Events) at Agra, India." *Environmental Science & Pollution Research* 20 (8): 5737–52.

Pope Francis I

Pope Francis I (1936–), born Jorge Mario Bergoglio, is a Roman Catholic pope known for being the first pope from the Americas and for his concern for poverty, sustainable development, the natural environment, social justice, ecumenism, and mercy. Born in Argentina, Francis entered the novitiate of the Society of Jesus (Jesuits) in 1958 and was ordained as a Catholic priest in 1969, after completion of his theological studies. During his novitiate years, he earned a master's-level degree in philosophy and taught literature and psychology at Jesuit preparatory high schools in Argentina. He was assigned to several official Jesuit leadership positions in the 1970s, became archbishop of Buenos Aires in 1998, and was created a cardinal by Pope John Paul II in 2001. In 2013 he was elected to the Roman Catholic papacy, and although he is the first Jesuit pope, he chose Francis as his papal name in honor of Francis of Assisi, a medieval Catholic saint known for embracing poverty, compassion for the poor, and love of all things in nature.

Pope Francis has addressed many important contemporary issues, with special emphasis on the importance of mercy and forgiveness, in his all papal letters, encyclicals, and interviews. He has upheld the Catholic Church's opposition to abortion, artificial contraception, and homosexuality but has repeatedly noted that God and Jesus offer forgiveness and mercy to everyone. Although Francis has emphasized forgiveness, he also publicly apologized in 2018 for the Church's extensive sexual abuse scandals. Regarding the ordination of women in the Catholic Church, Francis asserted the "door is closed" on both this issue and that of same-sex marriage, preferring to downplay their importance relative to other global issues. Francis has stated that poverty, inequality, greed, and respect for all of God's creation, including the natural environment, are the issues that are the most important for the Church and all of humanity to address. Additionally, to effectively address problems related to these global issues, it will require ecumenical and interreligious cooperation. As stated in Francis's papal writings and communications, it is only through this cooperation and God's mercy that homelessness, starvation, violence, inequality, injustice, and degradation of the natural environment will be overcome.

The natural environment, sustainable development, and social justice are all interrelated in the papal work of Francis. In 2015 he released the 184-page encyclical *Laudato Si': On Care for Our Common Home*, which calls for a global "ecological conversion" that includes commitment to environmental sustainability, preserving biological and cultural diversity, and implementing social justice. In other documents and statements, Francis has promoted environmental justice and expressed urgent concern for environmental degradation caused by human behaviors, including anthropogenic climate change, corporate greed, the placement of financial speculation over human needs, and the dehumanization of the poor. Some religious conservatives have criticized Francis's environmentalist statements as detracting from core teachings in Christianity, such as salvation through Jesus Christ and the centrality of the human person in God's creation. Others have expressed support for Francis's environmentalist approach, including many religious believers accepting it as good Christian stewardship and secular environmentalists welcoming support from an influential religious leader.

Numerous events, campaigns, projects, and discussions have been initiated because of Francis's insistence that *Laudato Si'* is "addressed to every person living on this planet." His papal commitment to environmental issues since 2013 has created interest and involvement globally. Annual conferences inspired by Francis's writings, such as the International Ecology Conference at Vatican City, bring together environmental activists and advocates, religious and political leaders, economists, scientists, and others to collaborate on cooperative global efforts. A campaign launched in 2018, the Catholic Climate Covenant, was inspired by Francis's environmental statements and collected eight hundred signatures from influential U.S. individuals and organizations that remained committed to the Paris Agreement on climate change regardless of the U.S. president's objections. Another example of Francis's influence is the 2019 "global synod" convened by the Vatican and Catholics around the world to protect the planet's forests, with the first stage of this effort focused on the forests of the Amazon. This "global synod" incorporates elements of contemporary digital media, including embedded social networking applications and a website with advocacy guidebooks, event planning guides, lesson plans, and many other tools to help achieve the campaign's goals.

See also: Environmental Justice; Francis of Assisi; *Laudato Si'*; Paris Agreement

Further Reading

Wall, Barbara E., and Massimo Faggioli, eds. 2019. *Pope Francis: A Voice for Mercy, Justice, Love, and Care for the Earth.* New York: Orbis Books.

R

Religious Environmental Movement

The religious environmental movement is a broad-based social movement that focuses on environmental issues from religious and spiritual perspectives. It has many philosophical and theological sources and involves many religious traditions globally. It consists of religious organizations and interest groups that share many goals with the secular environmental movement. Although it has roots in the contemporary secular environmental movement that emerged in the 1960s, the religious environmental movement did not formally emerge until the 1990s. The secular environmental movement provided a base of knowledge that includes strategies for mobilizing public support, organizing direct action, working with governments and policy agencies, and in general paving the way for acceptance or representation of environmental issues in local, regional, and global organizations. Because the religious environmental movement draws its membership and support from religious communities, issues in this movement are always presented in the ethical or theological framework of religious traditions. World religions, folk religions, nature religions, and Indigenous belief traditions have all contributed in some way to the emergence and rise of the religious environmental movement.

Initially, many religious adherents and secular environmentalists struggled to find common ground regarding beliefs and motivation. Some secular environmentalists believed that organized religion sought to dominate nature and encouraged behaviors that degrade or destroy the natural environment. Some religious institutions were concerned that secular environmentalists held views that were in opposition to various religious teachings, such as doctrines or practices involving reproduction, gender equality, and personhood. From the late 1960s to the present, different religions reviewed their sacred texts and practices with the hope of understanding the role of religion in environmental issues, including climate change, sustainability, pollution, and ecological degradation. By the 1980s many religious traditions globally were developing philosophical or theological guidelines for organized engagement of environmental issues. By the 1990s religious environmental organizations were being created, alliances were being formed among adherents from different belief systems and faith traditions, and a distinct religious environmental movement was emerging.

Throughout history, many religious traditions have had beliefs and practices that include a spiritual connection to the natural world, while others have placed more emphasis on the central importance of humanity. Some religions have sacred texts or practices that emphasize an interdependence among all living things and elements of creation. This emphasis on the interconnection of all life is often seen as a characteristic of Asian or Eastern religious traditions such Buddhism, Confucianism, Hinduism, Jainism, Shinto, Sikhism, and Daoism. The Abrahamic or monotheistic religions have been described by scholars and activists as anthropocentric, focusing on the relationship between humans and God and domination of nature by humans.

When the contemporary secular environmental movement began in the 1960s, many academics and activists believed that the Asian religious traditions, folk religions, and Indigenous belief systems included core beliefs and practices similar to those of the secular environmental movement, while the Abrahamic traditions were seen as allied with empire building, colonialism, and industrialism and were more inclined to dominate or ravage the natural world. In reality, the history of religions and the natural environment is extremely complex, with much variation by region, historical period, and circumstance within all religious traditions and belief systems. Despite having different approaches to the natural world, many religions globally had contributed to the emergence of a contemporary religious environmental movement by the 1990s.

Hinduism, as a religious tradition based in the Vedic texts and related cultural practices, has for centuries associated purity and sacredness with natural phenomena, such as the River Ganges and the sacred places it connects. Some scholars, such as the historian Lynn Townsend White Jr., have suggested that Asian religious traditions are inherently environmentalist. However, throughout most of its history, Hinduism in general viewed the material world and its problems as something to transcend but not necessarily resolve. One notable exception to this is the Bishnoi community, founded in the 1400s CE, whose members are devoted to a type of environmental conservation that prohibits the cutting of trees and killing of animals.

Inspired by the Bishnoi community, the more recent Chipko movement formed in 1973 to protest the felling of trees for a sports equipment factory. The Chipko movement eventually spread to other communities but was still a rare early example of religiously motivated environmentalism. Until recently, Hinduism emphasized the religious symbolism of the natural world rather than the more materialist approach found in environmental activism. Although the interdependence of all life and the sanctity of nature are important tenets of Hinduism, adherents of Hinduism have only recently begun, with some exceptions, to put their beliefs into practice as part of a religious environmental movement that shares goals with the secular environmental movement. By the late 1990s there was a significant increase in religiously motivated environmentalism within Hinduism.

Buddhism, although emerging from ancient Hinduism in India and having some shared or similar concepts and practices, has become a distinct global, diverse religious tradition involved in environmentalism. Many contemporary Buddhist scholars note a tension between ancient ideals and contemporary political action. Ancient Buddhist texts view the material world as a transient or impermanent condition from which individuals should seek to be liberated, while many contemporary Buddhists see social and political engagement as an essential element of the path to enlightenment. Although different Buddhist traditions clearly began recognizing the threat of industrialism to the natural environment by the beginning of the twentieth century, organized political engagement of environmental issues did not occur until after the 1960s as globalization spread the strategies, tactics, and networks of the secular environmental movement.

By the 1970s, for example, Buddhist conservation monks in Thailand were formally organizing to protect forests from multinational corporate logging. Similarly, the engaged Buddhism approach was shaping the beginnings of green Buddhism and eco-Buddhism in various Buddhist communities around the world. In recent decades, advances in communication and technology, including the internet and social media, have contributed to the emergence of an international Buddhism that connects many different traditions and interests. This international Buddhism draws inspiration from several different contemporary teachers and encourages social and political engagement at the local, regional, and global levels. Although grounded in ancient texts that clearly support a belief in the interdependence of all life and beings, Buddhism's involvement in environmentalism emerged after the distinct influences of the secular environmental movement, engaged Buddhism, and globalization.

Recognition of environmentalism as an important religious concern in the Abrahamic traditions of Judaism, Christianity, and Islam has followed a similar timeline to that of Asian religious traditions. Each of the Abrahamic traditions has many theological variations, but in general they focus theologically on the central importance of humans. In the late 1960s, the Judeo-Christian tradition specifically was criticized both for playing a major role historically in the destruction of the natural world and for its belief in humankind's divinely mandated domination of nature. Although many scholars and activists made similar accusations against the Judeo-Christian tradition, a 1967 article titled "The Historical Roots of Our Ecologic Crisis," by Lynn Townsend White Jr., was widely read throughout the late 1960s and well into the 1990s. Lynn Townsend White Jr.'s article is considered a flash point that prompted written responses, reflection, inquiry, and action in the Abrahamic traditions, and it continues to be cited today in many studies that examine religion and environmentalism.

In the late 1960s, the first and most numerous responses defending the Judeo-Christian tradition came from North American Jewish scholars. Orthodox Jewish scholars were the first to assert that criticisms were based on misunderstandings or mistranslations of religious texts and unfamiliarity with the Jewish tradition, but these Orthodox scholars were soon joined by thinkers from all branches of modern Judaism. In the 1970s a Jewish perspective emerged that addressed environmental issues, cited relevant Biblical and Talmudic sources, and suggested how Judaism might participate in environmentalism. From 1988 to 1995, the first known Jewish environmental organization, Shomrei Adamah, Keepers of the Earth, educated communities and published works about Jewish environmentalism, but did not focus their efforts on creating an action-oriented organization. By the 1990s, there were Jewish environmental organizations in Israel, such as the Herschel Center for Environmental Learning and Leadership, and in the United Kingdom, such as the Noah Project. However, the Coalition on the Environment and Jewish Life (COEJL), formed in 1992 in Washington, DC, is the organization that is most often credited with creating a unified Jewish environmental movement by adopting the strategies and expertise developed in the secular environmental movement.

Christianity's participation in the religious environmental movement occurred around the same time as Judaism's, with a few initial theological responses to criticisms of the Judeo-Christian tradition in the late 1960s and early 1970s. Many Christians, including laypersons, theologians, and clergy, initially avoided the secular environmental movement because of the movement's position on several social issues. In the 1970s a few Christian denominations made environmental statements but did not create related programs or suggest guidelines for Christian environmental action. There were some unsanctioned actions, such as members of religious orders participating in events to raise environmental awareness, but in general, Christian thinkers and theologians in the 1970s and 1980s focused on developing a specifically Christian approach to environmentalism.

Three dominant Christian approaches to environmentalism, those of stewardship, ecojustice, and creation spirituality, all emerged from the 1960s to the 1990s. For the most part during this time, Christian involvement in environmentalism occurred in North America and Europe but eventually spread around the world by the 1990s, as a majority of denominations began making official statements about environmental issues. When Christians did address environmental issues, environmental stewardship was the most common justification used by Evangelical, mainstream Protestant, Roman Catholic, and Orthodox churches. During the 1990s a distinct religious environmental movement within Christianity emerged, with organizations such as the Evangelical Environmental Network (EEN), Interfaith Power and Light (IPL), and various Catholic and Orthodox religious orders and lay groups formally organizing to enter political arenas and influence environmental policy in the name of a faith-based environmentalism.

Islam draws from some of the same stories, concepts, and ethical principles found in the sacred texts of Judaism and Christianity, although the Qur'an has a clearer emphasis on human responsibility regarding the natural environment. As with most other religious traditions, Muslim communities did not organize a specifically Islamic environmental movement until the 1990s. However, Islamic scholars in the twenty-first century refer to an Islamic Ecological Paradigm (IEP) that is based in the Qur'an and has explicitly influenced Muslims' relationship with the environment for more than 1,300 years. Although the term *IEP* was not used until the twenty-first century, by the 1980s Muslim philosophers and scholars were increasingly noting that there were shared values between Islam and modern environmentalism.

By the early 1990s Muslim scholars in the Arab world, the United Kingdom, and North America were framing environmental issues as part of a spiritual crisis requiring a response from Muslims. Grounding their actions in Qur'an texts that explicitly identify humans as caretakers of God's creation made for all generations and creatures, organizations emerged in the 1990s to address environmental issues and responsible stewardship of the earth from a Muslim perspective. The Islamic Foundation for Ecology and Environmental Sciences (IFEES), founded in 1994 in England, is one the earliest and most influential Islamic organizations in the religious environmental movement, with other organizations forming since then in Muslim communities around the world.

In addition to the Abrahamic and Asian religious traditions, there are many other religious and spiritual belief systems that also began focusing on environmental issues by the end of the twentieth century. Folk and Indigenous religions, usually associated with a specific region, ethnicity, tribe, or traditional knowledge, often have practices and beliefs that involve a close relationship with the natural environment. Some scholars and activists associate folk and Indigenous religions with traditional ecological knowledge (TEK) that promotes environmentalist values. In the twenty-first century, these folk and Indigenous religions, the Abrahamic and Asian religious traditions, and numerous newly emerging or reconstructed belief systems are all contributing in some way to the contemporary religious environmental movement. In the twenty-first century, religious traditions are increasingly applying their core beliefs and values to environmental issues, collaborating across traditions, and creating organizations that become part of the religious environmental movement.

See also: Buddhism; Christianity; Folk Religions; Hinduism; Islam; Judaism; Traditional Ecological Knowledge

Further Reading

Bell, Michael. 2018. *City of the Good: Nature, Religion, and the Ancient Search for What Is Right*. Princeton, NJ: Princeton University Press.
Ellingson, Stephen. 2016. *To Care for Creation: The Emergence of the Religious Environmental Movement*. Chicago and London: University of Chicago Press.
Gottlieb, Roger S. 2006. *A Greener Faith: Religious Environmentalism and Our Planet's Future*. New York: Oxford University Press.

Religious Naturalism

Religious naturalism is a philosophical approach that promotes leading a religious or spiritual life that is based in the belief that the natural world is the only reality. In this approach, religion and spirituality are grounded in scientific inquiry and rationality or scientific theories, such as evolution, but not in beliefs involving a supernatural God or gods, heaven, an afterlife, or a soul. Religious naturalists see humans and human civilization as emerging from and part of the natural world and use scientifically based narratives to explain the meaning and purpose of human life. They also assert that these explanatory narratives will change as scientific knowledge accumulates. Religious naturalists are often involved in the sciences and secular environmentalism, with a scientifically informed morality and set of values that are focused on ecological balance and social cooperation.

Religious naturalism is a form of philosophical naturalism, which is based on several premises and claims, including (1) only the natural world is real, (2) nature can be understood without appeal to a higher intelligence or purpose, (3) the natural world accounts for its own origin, and (4) every natural event is caused by other natural events. Some but not all philosophical naturalists additionally claim that science is the only method for achieving knowledge and that human interests are the only measure of value. Two essential characteristics found in most definitions of religious naturalism are (1) the belief that the natural world, including the cosmos, is the only reality and cause of events, and (2) a religious orientation focused on the natural world. This religious orientation does not include a belief in God, gods, or the supernatural, but it does include other religious elements, such as joy, wonder, humility, reverence, gratitude, and deep appreciation for life.

Religious naturalists assert that accurate explanations for the existence of the world do not need to include any supernatural forces or divine beings. Similarly, the world does not depend on guidance or maintenance provided by such supernatural beings or forces. All life and natural phenomena are sustained by the principles found in nature, both on Earth and throughout the cosmos. Meaning and purpose, as well as religious epiphany and ecstasy, are to be discovered and experienced by looking to the natural world instead of depending on a supernatural realm. Religious naturalism does share some characteristics with other environmentally oriented philosophies and theories, such as the Gaia hypothesis or the theology of Pierre Teilhard de Chardin. However, it does not include the debatable scientific claims of the Gaia hypothesis or a belief in the cosmic divinity suggested by Teilhard de Chardin. Although religious naturalism is usually not presented as being a solution to contemporary environmental issues, it is seen by some thinkers and activists as contributing to a deeper understanding of human interrelation with the rest of the natural world.

See also: Gaia Hypothesis; Teilhard de Chardin, Pierre

Further Reading

Stone, Jerome Arthur. 2017. *Sacred Nature: The Environmental Potential of Religious Naturalism*. London; New York: Routledge.

S

Shinto

Shinto is a religious tradition Indigenous to Japan based on beliefs and practices that have existed for thousands of years. With the arrival of Buddhism in Japan around 550 CE, Shinto became increasingly formalized and distinct from other religions. Shinto does not have a founder or sacred texts, and its primary focus is reverence of the *kami*, which are the spirits found in all things. Based on its focus on the natural world and belief that all things have a spirit, Shinto is considered a type of animism and a nature religion. Individual practice in Shinto includes worship, purification rituals, communion with the kami and ancestors, and recognizing nature as divine. During the 1800s Shinto was the official religion of Japan; it was enforced by the national government, which also controlled many of the kami shrines during that time. By the late 1940s the Japanese government no longer compelled its citizens to follow Shinto. Currently in Japan there are more than eighty thousand public shrines and an estimated eighty-five million followers of Shinto, with most involved through a localized practice of customs, beliefs, and rituals related to ancestors or kami.

In Shinto, nature is viewed as having spiritual and life-giving powers that manifest through all things in the natural world. There is a special emphasis on features of the landscapes, waterscapes, and the sky, or on individual objects such as a specific tree or boulder, as being places where kami reside. Rice cultivation and agriculture in general are associated with Shinto rituals and festivals, all of which developed over the centuries as interwoven parts of Indigenous Japanese lifestyles. Followers of Shinto place extreme importance on the preservation and maintenance of forests or groves, which serve as the locations and ritual spaces for kami shrines. Although the word *kami* is usually translated as god or deity, it is understood as a great power or spiritual quality that can bring happiness or misfortune, is beyond human capabilities, and resides in the elements and phenomena of the natural world.

In the twenty-first century, Shinto organizations and practitioners are involved in collaborative environmentalism. Although Shinto as a nature religion has historically encouraged environmentally friendly personal lifestyles, its followers have increasingly worked with other religions and secular international organizations on environmental projects and campaigns. For example, an international conference organized by Jinja Honcho (Association of Shinto Shrines) and the Alliance of Religions and Conservation (ARC) was held in 2014 at the sacred shrine of Ise. Formally titled "Tradition for the Future: Culture, Faith, and Values for a Sustainable Planet," this conference is one of many projects facilitated by ARC, Jinja Honcho, and others that disseminate information on environmentalism, emphasize Shinto as a model for nature-centered environmental sustainability, and encourage expansion of the global Green Pilgrimage Network (GPN).

See also: Alliance of Religions and Conservation; Animism; Green Pilgrimage Network; Nature Religions

Further Reading

Rots, Aike P. 2017. *Shinto, Nature and Ideology in Contemporary Japan: Making Sacred Forests*. London: Bloomsbury Publishing.

Shiva, Vandana

Vandana Shiva (1952–) is a physicist, environmental activist, and ecofeminist who focuses on food security and related issues. She was born in Dehradun, India, educated in India and Canada, and received a PhD in the philosophy of physics from the University of Western Ontario in 1978. Shiva became interested in environmental activism in the 1970s through her volunteer work with India's Chipko movement. In 1982, with the intent of creating a science learning center that includes Indigenous community knowledge, she founded the Research Foundation for Science, Technology and Ecology. In the late 1980s Shiva began a seed conservation network based in India that became Navdanya, an organization made up of farming families across India. Navdanya focused initially on farmers' rights and biodiversity conservation but has since expanded into related areas, including grassroots and research initiatives on agroecology, climate change, ecofeminism, organic farming, seeds, and soils. It also provides training in environmentalist advocacy and political literacy.

As an activist and author, Shiva asserts that biodiversity of seeds and soils are essential to all life and warns that corporate monocultures threaten this biodiversity. Much of her work emphasizes the importance of local communities with the traditional knowledge, skills, and motivation to strengthen biodiversity in agricultural practices. Additionally, Shiva's activism and writing gives special attention to women's roles in agriculture as well as their political involvement in an "Earth Democracy" based on biodiversity and cultural diversity. Shiva has led formal campaigns on issues such as genetic engineering of foods, corporate monoculture, food patents, and water privatization. Navdanya, under Shiva's direction, has been involved in related efforts, including legal claims against the World Trade Organization, World Bank, and various corporations regarding seed patents and infringement of intellectual property rights. In the twenty-first century, Navdanya and Shiva have continued to draw global attention to food security and related issues, such as the suicides of Indian farmers, GMOs and corporate seed monopolies, the marginalization of women, and the importance of women in conservation and environmentalism.

In *Religion and Sustainable Agriculture: World Spiritual Traditions and Food Ethics*, Shiva explains that her activism and writing are based in Hinduism, which teaches that food is a sacred gift of the earth, as are water, seeds, and soil. Shiva references ancient Vedic texts as the source of her belief that growing and sharing food are spiritual acts. She is also motivated by a belief in dharma, defined in Hinduism as the right way of living that involves all elements of the universe. The concept of dharma is essential to her ideas of food systems, which distinguish between those systems based on biodiversity, which create and maintain the web of life, and those based on ignorance and greed, which cause extinction and the collapse of ecosystems. Similarly, much of Shiva's most recent work includes an interest in how and why farmers in India and around the world are motivated to participate in sustainable agricultural practices because of religious beliefs, faith, rituals, and spiritual teachings.

See also: Biodiversity; Ecofeminism; Food Security; Hinduism; Soil Conservation

Further Reading

Astruc, Lionel. 2018. *Vandana Shiva: Creative Civil Disobedience.* Arles, France: Actes Sud.

LeVasseur, Todd, Pramod Parajuli, and Norman Wirzba, eds. 2016. *Religion and Sustainable Agriculture: World Spiritual Traditions and Food Ethics.* Lexington: University Press of Kentucky.

Sikhism

Sikhism is a religion that emerged in the Punjab region of India and Pakistan around 1500, with an estimated twenty-five million adherents globally by the early twenty-first century. Founded by Guru Nanak Dev Ji, Sikhism is monotheistic, emphasizes belief in karma and rebirth, and teaches that all humans must be treated as equals. Although Sikh scriptures use some Hindu terms, such as names and concepts from the Vedas, and acknowledge the Qur'an and the name of Allah from Islam, Sikhism is considered a distinct religion and not a merging of Hinduism and Islam. Sikhs believe that everything in the cosmos is interconnected and a manifestation of one God, who is the cause of all things. Sikhs aspire to total union with God, which can only be achieved through the law of karma, which determines the quality of an individual's life based on behavior in previous lives and provides for progression toward God by improvement through the cycle of rebirth.

As a strictly monotheistic religion, Sikhism asserts there is only one God that is both formless and genderless. All individuals, according to Sikhism, have direct access to God, are equal before God, must avoid empty religious rituals, and must live their lives in community with others. Although Sikhs believe that God is manifest inside everyone and that individual union with God is the most important goal, the ideal Sikh life is one of both union with God and service to others. Sikhism specifies three formal duties and five vices and provides instructions for living a good life that will bring individuals closer to union with God. The three duties are to pray, work, and give, all of which are to be done in service to others every day and with the recognition that the one God is manifest in all things. The five vices to be avoided are lust, greed, material attachment, anger, and pride, all of which are seen by Sikhs as separating them from their community and from God. Both the duties and vices are woven into Sikhism's ecological philosophy and religiously motivated environmentalism.

Sikhs believe that caring for the environment is essential to being in harmony with God and have worked with interreligious environmental organizations such the Alliance of Religions and Conservation (ARC). In 2009 Jathedar Gurbachan Singh, the head of the highest temporal and spiritual body of Sikhs, publicly stated that it is the "moral and religious duty" of each Sikh to actively care for the natural environment. In 2010 EcoSikh was formed to disseminate knowledge about environmental issues, including climate change and global warming, and to help Sikh communities around the world engage in environmental activism. Ongoing EcoSikh projects include the annual, global celebration of Sikh Environment Day, participation in the Green Pilgrimage Network (GPN), and the Green Gurdwaras campaign, which assists Sikhs in creating places of worship that are environmentally friendly and sustainable.

See also: Alliance of Religions and Conservation; Green Pilgrimage Network

Further Reading

Jhutti-Johal, Jagbir. 2011. *Sikhism Today*. New York: Continuum Publishing.

Socially Responsible Investment

Socially responsible investment (SRI) is a financial model that uses environmental, social and corporate governance criteria as a strategy for both generating financial returns and creating positive social impact. SRI is also referred to as ethical investing, green investing, sustainable investing, or values-based investing, and it attracts investors who believe that investments should contribute to social causes. Some examples include investments that positively impact human rights, community development, workplace safety, and corporate board diversity initiatives. SRI also encompasses many environmentally related investments such as water use, conservation, sustainable agricultural, clean energy and technology, climate change, and green construction. Types of SRI investors include individuals, families, retail companies, universities, retirement funds, religious organizations, and nonprofit organizations.

Many religious adherents have attempted to practice their values through financial activity for centuries. For thousands of years, ideal Vedic and Buddhist economic activity has been defined by the general tenets of do no harm, learn to do good, and purify the mind. Ancient Jewish texts suggest investing in ways that benefit the community long-term. The Catholic Church condemned exploitative lending practices as early as the thirteenth century. For hundreds of years Islam has used Halal financial guidelines that increasingly have emphasized socially responsible investment. More recently, the Society of Friends in the 1700s avoided financial interactions with any organizations or individuals involved in alcohol, gambling, the manufacturing of weapons, or the slave trade. In the 1920s Methodists in the United Kingdom refused to invest in "sin stocks" or "sin businesses" involved in alcohol, gambling, tobacco, sex, or slave labor. By the 1970s, many religions had developed internal guidelines specific to their traditions and global investment organizations, such as Pax World Fund and International Interfaith Investment Group, with the intent of using investments as a way to practice their values and beliefs.

Contemporary SRI financial groups use several strategies when working with religious investors, including screening and impact investing. Most religious organizations believe supporting environmental policy and programs is important, and they view impact investing as an effective way to integrate religious beliefs into investments and solve environmental challenges. Environmental impact investing identifies companies or financial opportunities that have a positive environmental impact, using screening methods to find a match with the goals or values of a specific religious investor.

The International Interfaith Investment Group (3iG) and the Interfaith Center on Corporate Responsibility (ICCR) are examples of the many agencies dedicated to connecting religious investors' funds with environmental causes. 3iG screens for investments and projects aligned with sustainable development, such as a reforestation program in Mozambique that will produce permanent income and jobs for communities in the region. ICCR has religious investment groups focused on climate change and water use, both of which identify challenges and opportunities in the private sector, and it works with industries to develop renewable energy sources, eliminate water contamination, and reduce water consumption in corporate water policies and supply chains.

See also: Alliance of Religions and Conservation

Further Reading

Budde, Scott J. 2008. *Compelling Returns: A Practical Guide to Socially Responsible Investing*. Hoboken, NJ: John Wiley & Sons.

Soil Conservation

Soil conservation refers to the processes, techniques, and strategies used to prevent the erosion and infertility of soil. Soil erosion results in loss of topsoil, which results in loss of nutrients needed for plant life and agricultural productivity. Soil erosion occurs when the soil is detached, moved, and then deposited at another location, taking with it both nutrients and contaminants. Causes of soil erosion include natural forces, such as water or wind, and agricultural practices such as tilling and slash-and-burn, which break apart soil structure and contribute to deforestation. Soil erosion can be accelerated by deforestation, which eliminates root systems that facilitate water drainage and removes trees that provide protective wind blocks. Causes of soil infertility include overuse, salination, acidification, and other types of chemical contamination through pesticides, herbicides, and fertilizers. Pesticides kill insects and organisms that are beneficial to soil structure and ecosystems; herbicides kill both weeds and beneficial plants; and fertilizers are often used to excess, eventually rendering the soil infertile or chemically unsuitable for plant and animal life. Soil conservation techniques used to prevent erosion and infertility include no-till farming, terrace farming, planting trees as windbreaks, crop rotation, composting, and the introduction of earthworms to provide fertilizer and create beneficial drainage.

The Soil Stewardship movement in the United States is one of the numerous examples of religiously motivated soil conservation efforts. The Soil Stewardship movement, which emerged in the 1930s as a response to the catastrophic effects of the Dust Bowl and the Great Depression, was founded on biblically based ideas about environmental stewardship. In the United States, soil erosion caused by the industrialization of agriculture and the increased use of intensive, unsustainable monocrop agriculture had become a national crisis by the early 1930s. By the mid-1930s, the U.S. government estimated that soil erosion, caused by unsustainable farming practices, drought, and wind, had ruined thirty-five million acres of land and damaged millions of additional acres.

During the 1930s, Protestant Christian farmers and religious leaders increasingly promoted farming as a Christian vocation that required sustainable stewardship of the earth. U.S. Christian farmers and their allies soon developed a biblically based response to the soil erosion crisis, and it was formally implemented by the 1940s. It included implementing Soil Stewardship Sunday and Soil Stewardship Week in U.S. churches and building formal relationships with government agencies that were promoting sustainable agriculture. The work of the Soil Stewardship movement continues in contemporary events such as Soil and Water Conservation Week, held annually in the United States. These events and initiatives are not always framed in religious language, and they are usually connected to state divisions of the National Association of Conservation Districts, a nonprofit organization dedicated to responsible use of natural resources.

Some soil conservationists are religiously motivated activists who are also scientifically trained and involved in sustainable farming initiatives and study centers. Vandana Shiva, a physicist, environmental activist, and ecofeminist, founded the seed conservation network and farm organization Navdanya, in India, and has been an advocate for soil conservation at the local, regional, and global level since the 1980s. Shiva's activism is rooted in Hinduism and ancient Vedic texts, which shape her belief that food, water, seeds, and soil are sacred gifts of the earth. For Shiva, practicing soil conservation is both a spiritual act and essential for creating and maintaining the web of life.

In her 2016 book, *Soil Not Oil*, Shiva asserts that "soil, not oil, offers a framework for converting the ecological catastrophe and human brutalization we face into an opportunity to reclaim our humanity and our future." Bringing together scientific research, social analysis, and Hindu spirituality, Shiva writes that the "most creative and necessary work that humans do is to work with the soil as co-producers of nature." In both her writing and her activism, she also asserts that soil fertility is essential for mitigating and adapting to climate change. At the Navdanya farm, participants have practiced and studied soil conservation for decades, creating fertile soil by nurturing live microorganisms, including earthworms and fungi. Shiva and her colleagues share their research and vision of soil conservation locally and internationally with scientists, soil conservationists, environmentalists, government agencies, and universities.

In addition to grassroots movements and influential activists, a connection between religion and soil conservation is found in education and research organizations that collect, sponsor, and disseminate information on soil conservation and related topics. EcoMENA is a source of expertise on all aspects of the Middle East and North Africa environmental sectors, providing advisory, project management, workshops, publishing, marketing, and publicly accessible online archives. Although EcoMENA focuses on disseminating scientific research, many of the contributors and countries involved in its initiatives are governed by Islamic law, so religious values are often implicit rather than explicit in EcoMENA's mission. EcoMENA is managed and supported by volunteers, and although most of their research and initiatives cover the Middle East and North Africa, their primary goal is to create public environmental awareness and to foster sustainability globally. The countries that participate in EcoMENA include Qatar, Saudi Arabia, Bahrain, Kuwait, Oman, United Arab Emirates, Jordan, Iraq, Egypt, Palestine, Lebanon, Morocco, and Tunisia. EcoMENA's recent initiatives in soil conservation in these member countries include bioremediation research, composting in Qatar, vermicomposting, irrigation systems in the Middle East, and many other related issues and topics. The Heschel Center for Sustainability (HCS) in Israel is another of the many examples of organizations that focus on a specific region and are influenced by the connection between religion and environmental issues. HCS is a leading advocate for a sustainable Israel and offers educational programs, sponsors research, supports sustainability policy, and integrates soil conservation practices into many of its initiatives.

See also: Climate Change; Deforestation; Food Security; Shiva, Vandana; Sustainability

Further Reading

Lowe, Kevin M. 2016. *Baptized with the Soil: Christian Agrarians and the Crusade for Rural America.* Oxford: Oxford University Press.
Shiva, Vandana. 2016. *Soil Not Oil: Climate Change, Peak Oil and Food Insecurity.* London: Zed Books.

Sustainability

Sustainability is the ability of a society, ecosystem, or habitat to meet the needs of its current population without putting future generations at risk. Carrying capacity, an essential factor of environmental sustainability, refers to the population size that can be sustained or supported indefinitely by a specific habitat, ecosystem, or society. The presence of renewable resources and the amount of waste generated are two additional essential factors used to calculate the sustainability of a society, habitat, or ecosystem. Sustainable development is an important element of environmental sustainability as well, and includes planning of communities, population projections, availability and anticipated use of natural resources, and preservation of wilderness areas. The earth's numerous habitats, ecosystems, and societies are interdependent parts of a larger planetary ecosystem, in which changes in one ecosystem or region affect the sustainability of other ecosystems. Currently, scientists have identified several major threats to the sustainability of the planetary ecosystem and its smaller interdependent ecosystems. These threats are usually measured in terms of thresholds, tipping points, and planetary boundaries, and include climate change, biodiversity loss, ocean acidification, land use, biochemical, pollution, fresh water, atmospheric aerosols, and ozone depletion.

The World Council of Churches (WCC) was one of the first religious organizations to discuss sustainability. It occurred at the 1974 WCC Church and Society Conference on Science and Technology for Human Development, held in conjunction with the UN Conference on World Population. At the end of the conference, the WCC and other participants declared that any policies related to world population should have the goal of "a robust, sustainable society." Soon after, at their 1975 meeting in Nairobi, the WCC Assembly included the phrase "just, participatory, and sustainable society" in the goals listed in their formal mission statement. In the following decades, several religious traditions defined sustainability as part of their ethical and moral responsibility, with each tradition interpreting sustainability through its sacred texts, oral traditions, or practices. Additionally, many religious traditions assert that environmental justice is an essential element of sustainability.

By 2020 many religions developed formal strategies to engage both their adherents and global civil society in sustainability, often focusing on sustainable development. Islamic Relief sponsored the 2019 conference on "Religion and Sustainable Development: Building Partnerships to End Extreme Poverty" conference, which included the World Bank Group and numerous government agencies, religious organizations, and academic institutions. In 2019 the Vatican sponsored a similar conference titled "Religions and the Sustainable Development Goals [SDGs]: Listening to the Cry of the Earth and of the Poor," with the intent to "marshal the moral force of religion behind the implementation of the SDGs." These conferences, along with numerous other events, projects, and policies sponsored by the world's religions, increasingly focus on meeting the SDGs established in the UN 2030 Agenda for Sustainable Development.

Some religious organizations that support the sustainability goals of global institutions have been practicing religiously motivated sustainability for several decades in communities around the world. Founded in 1995 in Santiago, Cuba, the Centro Cristiano Lavastida de Servicio y Capacitación (Lavastida Christian Center for Service and Training) is an example of a regional religious organization that is committed to environmental sustainability that meets the specific needs of the communities it serves. The Centro, an ecumenical center with historical connections to the WCC and the Cuban Council of Churches, promotes sustainability through agroecology and permaculture, and provides related training programs and social services in Santiago and Cuba's other eastern cities. The Centro's mission also includes working collaboratively on sustainability initiatives with other nongovernmental organizations (NGOs), government agencies, international movements, and various religious traditions.

Additionally, the Centro's training program promotes environmental sustainability in regional churches in several ways, including conducting workshops, publishing an annual journal of ecotheology, and sponsoring an annual Forum on Ecology. Researchers, church leaders, and individuals involved in sustainability projects are among the participants at the annual Forum, which provides a venue for sharing experiences, research, and ideas. The Centro's Social Services Program has four divisions that focus on ecology, agroecology, permaculture, and food conservation, with each division having promoters and project leaders. The ecology division organizes community projects, such as gardening and recycling trash, while the agroecology division provides training in sustainable food production. The permaculture division integrates agroecology into all areas of community life, including sustainable housing and creating harmonious relationships between humans and the natural environment. The food conservation division provides services that are especially helpful in times of crisis, such as when Hurricane Sandy devasted the region in 2012. The leaders from all areas of the Social Services Program regularly work together to provide training, services, resources, and outreach to communities, combining religious beliefs with activism.

A Rocha Kenya (ARK) is among the many global examples of communities adopting and practicing religiously motivated sustainability.

ARK, an interdenominational Christian organization, has been a registered nongovernmental organization in Kenya since 1999 and is Kenya's oldest environmental, faith-based organization. In Kenya, where 80 percent of the population identifies as Christian, ARK's religiously motivated environmentalism and sustainability initiatives have been well received by much of the population. ARK, located in Watamu, near the Indian Ocean, focuses on sustainability, habitat conservation, community engagement, and environmental education, with all of its initiatives incorporating its five values, which are Christian, Conservation, Community Outreach, Cross-Cultural, and Cooperation. ARK's Arabuko-Sokoke schools and Ecotourism scheme (ASSETS) program supports ecotourism and conservation; works with the Kenya Wildlife Service, Kenya Ministry of Education, and the UN; and provides secondary school scholarships for local children. The Dakatcha Woodland project introduced a sustainable agriculture model called "Farming God's Way," which addresses food security issues in the communities bordering the woodlands and teaches biblically based environmental stewardship.

Projects that are representative of ARK's ecological science initiatives include the Kenya Bird Map project, in collaboration with the National Museums of Kenya, the University of Cape Town, and others, and the Hawkfish Ecology project, which sponsors research on coral reefs in Watamu Marine National Park. ARK's Tana River Delta project works to provide sustainable alternatives to proposed sugarcane plantations and woodlands biofuel harvesting. ARK's alternatives prevent destruction of the regional ecosystems and prevent displacement of the local cattle herders. In addition to supporting scientific research and expanding ecotourism, ARK's religiously motivated sustainability efforts have increased educational opportunities for local communities, trained local children and adults as citizen-scientists, and defined environmental sustainability as service to God and God's creation.

While many communities have been practicing environmental sustainability for innumerable generations as part of their spirituality and traditional ecological knowledge (TEK), many of the world's religions have only recently integrated environmental sustainability into their core beliefs and practices. By examining their sacred texts, oral traditions, and spiritual practices, religious leaders have discovered that supporting environmental sustainability through education, conservation, activism, and policy is a moral obligation. At the national and global levels, leaders of the world's religions shape policy and make formal statements that provide guidance for religious believers. Organizations such as the WCC provide opportunities for religious organizations to interact with scientists, experts, and policy advisers, and to learn new strategies for supporting religiously motivated environmental sustainability. At the local and regional levels, communities are increasingly implementing religiously motivated sustainability initiatives that are rooted in their religious beliefs, serve the specific needs of their people, and protect their ecosystems.

See also: Biodiversity; Deforestation; Environmental Justice; Food Security; Marine Conservation; Traditional Ecological Knowledge; World Council of Churches

Further Reading

Caraway, Rose T. 2018. "Religion, Sustainability Movements, and Ecumenism: A Case Study in Santiago de Cuba." *Journal for the Study of Religion, Nature and Culture* 12 (4): 438–65.

Johnston, Lucas F. 2014. *Religion and Sustainability: Social Movements and the Politics of the Environment*. Hoboken, NJ: Routledge.

LeVasseur, Todd, Pramod Parajuli, and Norman Wirzba, eds. 2016. *Religion and Sustainable Agriculture: World Spiritual Traditions and Food Ethics*. Lexington: University Press of Kentucky

Moyer, Joanne. 2015. "Faith-Based Sustainability in Practice: Case Studies from Kenya." *Journal for the Study of Religion, Nature and Culture* 9 (1): 42–67.

Tomalin, Emma, Jörg Haustein, and Shabaana Kidy. 2019. "Religion and the Sustainable Development Goals." *Review of Faith and International Affairs* 17 (2): 102–18.

T

Teilhard de Chardin, Pierre

Pierre Teilhard de Chardin (1881–1955) was a paleontologist, geologist, Jesuit priest, and mystic who conducted scientific field research, taught at universities, and wrote extensively on evolution and spirituality. Teilhard was born in France and educated in England and France, and he held teaching positions in several countries. He was eventually banned from teaching by the Jesuit Order because the Catholic Church believed he was denying the doctrine of original sin. Although Teilhard was ordained a priest in the Jesuit Order in 1911, he served in the French military during WWI as a stretcher-bearer. Beginning in the 1920s, Teilhard conducted paleontological work in China, South America, and Africa. He was a prolific writer in several areas, including scientific research and thought, philosophy of science, and Christian theology, although many of works were censored by the Jesuit Order and the Catholic Church. He is considered one of the primary inspirations for ecotheology, which is a theological approach focusing on religion, nature, and environmentalism.

In the 1930s Teilhard wrote extensively on evolution and science in *The Phenomenon of Man*, a book that was not published until 1955 due to censure by the Catholic Church. In this book and other writings, Teilhard asserts that planetary history and human evolution are essential elements of what he calls the Omega Point, which is the final point of divine unification of all things in the universe. All life throughout time, from the smallest cells to primordial plants to more complex living creatures are part of a divinely planned evolution that culminates in all things merging with the Cosmic Christ at the Omega Point. In the *Phenomenon of Man*, Teilhard also fully developed his concept of the noösphere. The earth, according to Teilhard, has evolved in distinct layers over time, starting with the geosphere, then the biosphere, then the noösphere, and it will ultimately develop a theosphere in the future. He asserted that the planet's currently evolving layer is the noösphere, or layer of mind and spirit, which is the collective emergence of all human thought. Another important element of human evolution toward the Omega Point is Teilhard's idea that love is essential for the survival and salvation of humanity. He further believed that this love must be directed at all living things as part of a divinely mandated interdependence.

Most of Teilhard's writings were not published until after his death in 1955. The Roman Catholic Church continued to censure him and ban his writing from seminary libraries, religious schools, and Catholic bookstores for several years. However, by the late 1960s, during the Second Vatican Council, there was an interest in understanding Christ in a cosmological sense. Beginning in the 1960s several prominent theologians wrote defenses of Teilhard's cosmic theology, which by the 1980s had been approved and referenced by many leaders in the Roman Catholic Church. During this time, responses from the scientific community were varied, with some scientists refusing to acknowledge any scientific value in Teilhard's theories and other scientists noting that Teilhard's evolutionary theory offered important insights into human evolutionary development and humankind's relation to nature.

By the end of the twentieth century, Teilhard's writings were considered seminal in the research and scholarship of several fields, including conservation ecology, ecotheology, and theoretical studies of the internet's social dimensions. In the twenty-first century, Roman Catholic Church authorities, including both Pope Benedict XVI and Pope Francis I, have recognized Teilhard as extremely influential and visionary. Within the Jesuit Order, Teilhard's writings have been incorporated into spiritual retreats that frame ecological destruction as a spiritual crisis resulting from a dysfunctional relationship between humans and God. These retreats teach that the earth and the natural environment are imbued with God's presence and have the capacity to heal the relationship between humans and God.

Teilhard wrote both as a religious mystic and a scientist, and created a cosmic theology grounded in Christian beliefs and his paleontological research. In this cosmic theology, the physical and the spiritual evolution of humanity is interdependent with all other life, and love is essential to the survival and salvation of humanity. Teilhard also suggests throughout much of his theological writing that human greed and exploitation are the primary causes of environmental destruction. As part of evolution toward the Omega Point, Teilhard urged humankind to change its attitude and cultivate reverence for the natural world created by God. Framed in theological language that focuses on a Cosmic Christ and the role of humans in the evolutionary progress of the earth, Teilhard's emphasis on the interdependence of all living things was extremely influential in the eventual emergence of ecotheology, as well as in several other fields involved in environmentalism.

See also: Ecotheology; Gaia Hypothesis

Further Reading

Deane-Drummond, Celia. 2006. *Pierre Teilhard de Chardin on People and Planet.* London and Oakville, CT: Equinox.

Meynard, Thierry, ed. 2006. *Teilhard and the Future of Humanity.* New York: Fordham University Press.

Teilhard de Chardin, Pierre. 2002. *The Phenomenon of Man.* New York: Perennial Library.

Traditional Ecological Knowledge

Traditional ecological knowledge (TEK) refers to a cultural group's knowledge, practices, and beliefs related to their habitat or ecosystem. The term came into widespread use in the 1980s, when anthropologists began emphasizing the ecological importance of a community's lived experiences with their natural environment, as well as how those experiences become expert knowledge that is culturally transmitted over generations. As a research term, TEK was initially used to reference Indigenous knowledge, but it expanded over time to encompass all aspects of any group's persistent knowledge of its natural environment. The TEK of a group or community includes the stories and symbolism associated with animals, plants, and natural landscapes that are found in the region inhabited by those people. TEK also includes any rituals, ceremonies, and food or medicine practices that have developed through interaction with the natural environment. In current academic research, the TEK of a group or subculture includes the following: factual observations, resource management strategies, an understanding of past uses of local land and resources, values regarding the natural environment, cultural identity tied to place or landscapes, and a cosmology that explains how all things in the ecosystem are connected.

In the twenty-first century, the term *traditional ecological knowledge* (TEK) is used in the social sciences, conservation science, health and medicine, and religious studies, as well as in environmentalist discussions. Additionally, governments, health-care systems, universities, and other organizations seek out TEK that can provide insights about the natural environment that are not accessible through mainstream research or Western science. National park systems around the world, for example, have begun formally incorporating the TEK of tribal elders into wildlife and forest management programs. Similarly, health-care systems have been including the TEK of Indigenous elders in patient treatments and preventative nutrition, medical school training, and family support services. TEK is also incorporated into the study of religion and environmentalism, both as an analytical concept and as a source of invaluable information on the spiritual or religious relationship of a community with its surrounding natural environment.

As an analytical concept, TEK provides a method for identifying a community's knowledge, beliefs, and practices involving its ecosystem or natural environment. The concept of TEK is also used to distinguish this traditional knowledge from scientifically acquired knowledge. As a type of traditional knowledge, TEK accumulates over many generations of people who have lived in a specific place or ecosystem and includes the properties of plants, the habits of wildlife, the weather cycles, and astronomical and geological phenomena. TEK is interwoven into the religious or spiritual practices, values, and beliefs of the community, which often emphasize the interdependence among all things in the community's ecosystem.

TEK, both as a concept and a type of data, is found in studies on world religions, folk religions, and new religious movements. Examples of TEK used in the study of world religions include researching the conservation practices of Buddhist communities in the Himalayas and documenting the eco-Islamic movement's emphasis on the shared goals of global secular organizations and on local Qur'an-based environmental stewardship. TEK is also used in research on Neo-paganism and nature religions, such as Druidry or Wicca, which rely on folk ecological knowledge, emphasize environmental sustainability, and promote conservation in local, regional, and national politics.

See also: Folk Religions; Nature Religions; Paganism

Further Reading

Nelson, Melissa K., and Dan Shilling. 2018. *Traditional Ecological Knowledge: Learning from Indigenous Practices for Environmental Sustainability*. New Directions in Sustainability and Society. Cambridge and New York: Cambridge University Press.

V

Vegetarianism

Vegetarianism refers to the practice of eating only plants and plant-based foods, and excluding flesh and animal-based foods from daily diets. There are several recognized variations, such as lacto-vegetarians who include dairy, ovo-vegetarians who include eggs, and vegans who do not consume any products derived from animals. The recorded history of vegetarianism goes back to around 1500 BCE, in ancient India, although it is likely that vegetarianism was practiced much earlier in various cultures either out of necessity or because of spiritual beliefs. Previous to the twentieth century, vegetarianism was usually practiced because of religious beliefs, although there have been numerous philosophers who were advocates of ethical vegetarianism. Beginning in the 1970s, Peter Singer and other ethical philosophers argued for vegetarianism and animal rights based on ethical and moral grounds rather than religious beliefs. Although estimates vary, in 2018 around 20 percent of the world's population was practicing some form of vegetarianism, with a majority being vegetarian by necessity. Although promoted as part of a healthy lifestyle in some societies, vegetarianism by choice is often practiced for spiritual, religious, or ethical reasons having to do with both animal rights and the environmental impact of producing animal-based foods.

Driven by arguments in favor of rights for animals as sentient beings, vegetarianism based solely on ethical grounds has increased significantly in recent decades, primarily in high-income countries around the world. Vegetarianism based on religious beliefs has a much longer history, going back thousands of years in some traditions. Several religious traditions have only recently discovered or emphasized vegetarianism as a religious practice, influenced by environmental issues such as climate change and sustainability, advances in health and nutritional sciences, and concerns related to animal welfare.

Religions that have been and continue to be strong advocates of vegetarianism include Jainism, Hinduism, and Buddhism, all of which originated in ancient India. Vegetarianism is required of Jains, based on their core beliefs of nonviolence, karma, and rebirth. Jains define killing animals as intentional violence that prevents spiritual attainment or enlightenment. In Hinduism and Buddhism, vegetarianism based in nonviolence and karma is supported by some sacred texts and important religious leaders, and it is practiced by many followers but is not mandatory. In the Abrahamic religions, Judaism as a whole has increasingly advocated vegetarianism since the early 1900s, while a few groups in both Christianity and Islam have only recently begun promoting vegetarianism. There are some exceptions, such as Seventh-Day Adventists in Christianity, but overall, vegetarianism in the Abrahamic traditions has been the exception rather than the rule.

Increasingly, groups and leaders within both Judaism and Christianity as well as other religions are becoming strong advocates of vegetarianism, for various reasons. In general, Jewish vegetarianism is grounded in a concern for animals and in the belief that God intended humans to be vegetarian. In Christianity, vegetarianism is usually practiced as a type of religious fasting or for improved health rather than for animal welfare concerns. Historically, there have been several rabbis and philosophers in Judaism that recommended vegetarianism, such as Nachmanides (1194–1270 CE) and Joseph Albo (1380–1444 CE), but it was relatively recently that a modern Jewish vegetarian movement emerged. Nachmanides asserted that all "living creatures possess a moving soul and a certain spiritual superiority": Albo noted that "in the killing of animals there is cruelty, rage" and "shedding of innocent blood": and they both taught that vegetarianism is God's dietary ideal. However, it was not until the late nineteenth century that these ideas began to gather widespread support, and by the late twentieth century, they developed into a distinctly Judaic approach to vegetarianism.

Contemporary Jewish writers and leaders who are advocates for vegetarianism argue that it is firmly based in the sacred texts and spiritual tradition of Judaism. In 1986 Rabbi Arthur Hertzberg, in his contribution to the Assisi Declarations, wrote that Judaism must move collectively toward vegetarianism as "the ultimate mean of the Jewish moral teaching." Similarly, Rabbi David Rosen stated in 2018 that "animal products in global industrialized food production are all in contravention of Jewish teaching." In the past and currently, the reasons given for vegetarianism in Judaism are that, as stated in the Torah, God prefers that humans eat plants; God allows meat-eating only as a concession to human choice or desire; and the Torah forbids human cruelty and violence that cause animal suffering.

In Christianity there are a few groups and leaders who are strong advocates of religiously motivated vegetarianism as a healthy, biblically supported diet, but there is no distinct, unified Christian vegetarian movement. The Seventh-Day Adventist Church, founded in 1863, has continuously taught that vegetarianism is an important option for a healthy life and for being human examples of God's love and care. In 2018 the Seventh-Day Adventist Church reported having more than twenty million members globally, with a majority practicing some form of vegetarianism, which is strongly encouraged but not mandatory. Other contemporary advocates of Christian vegetarianism include Franklin Graham, son of the influential evangelical leader Billy Graham, and Rick Warren, author of *The Purpose Driven Life* and evangelical pastor.

Both Graham and Warren, along with many Evangelical Protestants in the United States, support the "Daniel Fast" and the "Daniel Plan," which are based on the biblical Book of Daniel. The Daniel Fast is a plant-based diet intended to bring Christians closer to God by avoiding the consumption of meat, and it provides guidance by emphasizing faith, food, fitness, focus, and friends. Although most religiously motivated Christian vegetarianism focuses on individual health or religious fasting, there are examples of Christian vegetarianism based on environmental stewardship, nonviolence, and compassion. Francis of Assisi (c. 1181–1226) practiced vegetarianism out of compassion and love, and contemporary Christian organizations that advocate vegetarianism based on stewardship of God's creation include the international Christian Vegetarian Association and Catholic Concern for Animals.

See also: Assisi Declarations; Buddhism; Climate Change; Hinduism; Jainism; Sustainability

Further Reading

Labendz, Jacob Ari, and Shmuly Yanklowitz, eds. 2019. *Jewish Veganism and Vegetarianism: Studies and New Directions*. Albany: State University of New York Press.

Linzey, Andrew, and Clair Linzey. 2018. *Ethical Vegetarianism and Veganism*. Abingdon, UK: Routledge.

Stewart, James John. 2018. *Vegetarianism and Animal Ethics in Contemporary Buddhism*. London: Routledge.

Walters, Kerry S., and Lisa Portmess. 2001. *Religious Vegetarianism: From Hesiod to the Dalai Lama*. Albany: State University of New York Press.

Water

Water is essential for all life and is at the center of environmental issues, including climate change, drought, deforestation, flood management, energy and food production, and sanitation. These and other issues, such as water quality, water rights, and water supply and management, are creating a sense of urgency as human populations place increasing demands on the planet's finite water sources. There are numerous factors contributing to the world's emerging water crisis. Climate change is creating drought in some areas and flooding in others, which results in forced migration, conflict, and health issues. The human population is increasing, which increases the demand for water. The world's overall income level is increasing, which has led to increased consumption of water-intensive products such as animal-based foods and fossil fuels. Water issues in the twenty-first century are further complicated by outdated or deteriorating water infrastructures, including canals, treatment plants, pipes, and sewer systems. Additionally, natural infrastructures, such as trees, forests, extensive root systems, and robust soils that buffer, filter, and regulate rainwater and groundwater, are all currently underutilized in water management. Because it is an urgent global issue, the UN has declared that ensuring "availability and sustainable management of water and sanitation for all" is one of the sustainable development goals (SDG 6) for 2030. Water is considered essential to sustainable development in general, with health, education, economics, and the environment all dependent on safe and accessible water supplies.

Most religions, including Indigenous spiritual traditions, believe water is sacred and include it in their ceremonies and rituals. Water is at the center of purification rituals in Hinduism, Shinto, Judaism, Christianity, Islam, Sikhism, and numerous other religious traditions. Additionally, many religious traditions view culturally significant bodies of water as sacred or believe that deities reside in bodies of water. Most religious traditions include instructions about water and its use, which inform cultural practices that help mitigate the potentially alienating effects of modern water policies. Because of their reverence of water, both as an abstract symbol of life and as a life-giving natural resource in communities and ecosystems, religious traditions have important roles to play in the developing global water crisis.

Religious traditions and their leaders have influence that transcends the ideological, jurisdictional, institutional, and economic boundaries that often impede attempts to resolve issues and challenges involving water. Members of religious traditions often cross these boundaries to stand in solidarity with marginalized communities experiencing water deprivation or to help mediate contentious water policies. In recent years, religious leaders have increasingly collaborated on interreligious efforts to address global water issues, for example, participating in UNESCO's 2003 World Water Forum in Kyoto and the subsequent UNESCO Water and Ethics research series. Representatives from diverse religious traditions also collaborate on current initiatives such as World Water Week, which is sponsored by the World Council of Churches (WCC) and other organizations, and focuses on water issues and the UN SDG 6.

There are clear examples of competition over water resources that involve conflict between religious traditions, such as water disputes between Palestine and Israel, Iraq and Syria, and India and Pakistan. However, interreligious cooperation on water issues is increasing. In addition to religious leaders collaborating on global initiatives sponsored by the UN and other international organizations, there are numerous interreligious and ecumenical initiatives addressing water issues. The WCC's Ecumenical Water Network (EWN) is an example of cooperation on water issues among different branches of Christianity. The EWN provides information to Christian organizations and individuals about the global water crisis and offers community-based solutions, while also being a strong advocate for the human right to water. Since 2008, EWN has sponsored Seven Weeks for Water, which is celebrated globally by the WCC member churches. Each year, Seven Weeks for Water focuses on a different region and theme, such as the 2019 focus on Asia, gender, and water issues. EWN also participates in annual events sponsored by the UN Inter-Agency Task Force on Religion and Development (UNIATF) and contributes to international events, such as the 2018 Alternative World Water Forum (Forum Alternativo Mundial da Agua) held in Brazil.

Another example of interreligious cooperation on water issues is the Global Interfaith Wash Alliance (GIWA), which advocates for clean water, sanitation, and hygiene for all, with a regional focus on India and contiguous nations. Since its inception in 2013, GIWA has brought together followers of several traditions, including Judaism, Jainism, Christianity, Hinduism, Buddhism, Sanathan Dharma, Vaishnavism, and Hare Krishna, to achieve these goals. GIWA asserts that religious and spiritual traditions provide the inspiration and motivation that help people learn and implement new behaviors, including those involving water use, and provides leaders in these traditions with relevant education, skills, and supplies. Religious and spiritual leaders are also encouraged to collaborate with governments, businesses, and civil society in general to achieve GIWA's goals.

GIWA's formal partners include the United Religions Initiative, the International Partnership on Religion and Sustainable Development, the World Wide Fund for Nature (formerly World Wildlife Fund [WWF]), EcoPeace Middle East, UNICEF, USAID, and numerous other nongovernmental and governmental organizations. Several of GIWA's ongoing programs focus on education, including WASH on Wheels, which travels around India educating villages about sanitation and water conservation; World Toilet College, which offers classes on toilet building and household sanitation; Water School, which teaches sustainable water management; and rural workshops on handwashing and toothbrush use. Additionally, GIWA provides training on bio-sand water filters and water sanitizing, teaches women entrepreneurial skills, and provides disaster relief in India and Nepal.

Almost every religious tradition has organizations that are focused on the contemporary water challenges and issues experienced by its followers. The Jewish National Fund (JNF), founded in 1901 to reestablish a Jewish homeland in Israel, is an example of an organization focused on the environmental challenges experienced by the members of a specific religious tradition. JNF is a UN nongovernmental organization and is currently involved in building sustainable communities in Israel's deserts, rehabilitating rivers, conducting water research, developing energy sources, and numerous other initiatives. As part of building sustainable communities, JNF has planted millions of trees, increased Israel's water supply, and developed agricultural practices for Israel's arid climate.

Water is an essential element of sustainable communities, and much of JNF's work focuses on strengthening Israel's water economy, including developing alternative water sources, innovating irrigation practices, and discovering methods to improve water quality. Additionally, because

Israel's population and demand for water are continuously increasing, JNF prioritizes initiatives that increase sustainable water resources. JNF has met Israel's growing demand for water by expanding water treatment and recycling facilities, collecting runoff and waste water, restoring damaged river systems, and building more than 250 reservoirs as of 2019. Additionally, JNF builds sewage purification facilities to treat regional wastewater for agricultural use, and it sponsors many of Israel's water awareness educational programs. One of these programs, JNF's Rainwater Harvesting system, has been installed in more than fifty of Israel's schools and provides young people the opportunity to construct and maintain functioning water systems.

There are thousands of diverse Indigenous groups around the world, and most of them honor water as an essential element of their spirituality and traditional ecological knowledge (TEK). Many Indigenous groups belief they have a sacred responsibility to protect water and its sources and are involved in activism focused on water and related issues.

In North America, Honor the Earth and Water Protectors are examples of two Indigenous environmentalist groups that are actively involved in conserving and protecting natural water sources. Honor the Earth (HTE) was founded in 1993 by Indigenous activist Winona LaDuke and the musical duo Indigo Girls as an organization focused on both Indigenous struggles and environmental justice.

Most of HTE's environmentalist initiatives, including their work related to water, are in Minnesota and its neighboring states. Examples of HTE's numerous water initiatives include prevention of invasive aquatic species and opposition to extraction operations, such as hydraulic fracturing, mining, and gas and petroleum pipelines, that contaminate water sources and destroy ecosystems. Additionally, HTE collaborates with environmentalist groups such as Water Protectors, a North American Indigenous environmentalist network committed to protecting the earth's water. Both HTE and Water Protectors have stated that their water activism must be nonviolent and based in traditional ecological knowledge (TEK), Indigenous spiritual knowledge, and reverence for Mother Earth.

Recent legislation in New Zealand provides another example of the convergence of environmentalism and Indigenous spiritual knowledge. For several years the Whanganui Iwi Maori people campaigned for national legislation, finally passed in 2017 by the New Zealand government, that gave the Whanganui River status as a legal person. The Whanganui people believe that the Whanganui River and other rivers

are their ancestors as well as a source of both physical and spiritual sustenance, and therefore they must be given the same types of rights and pro-
tections as humans.

See also: Climate Change; Deforestation; Hydraulic Fracturing; Traditional Ecological Knowledge; World Council of Churches

Further Reading

Chamberlain, Gary. 2008. *Troubled Waters: Religion, Ethics, and the Global
Water Crisis.* Lanham, MD: Rowman & Littlefield.

McAnally, Elizabeth. 2019. *Loving Water across Religions: Contributions to an
Integral Water Ethic.* Maryknoll, NY: Orbis Books.

UNESCO, and the International Council of Monuments and Sites. 2015. *Water
& Heritage: Material, Conceptual and Spiritual Connections.* Edited by
W. J. H. Willems and Henk P. J. van Schaik. Leiden, Netherlands: Sidestone
Press.

World Health Organization, and UNICEF. 2017. *Progress on Drinking Water,
Sanitation and Hygiene: 2017 Update and SDG Baselines.* Geneva, Switzerland:
World Health Organization and the United Nations Children's Fund.

White, Lynn Townsend, Jr.

Lynn Townsend White Jr. (1907–1987) was a historian who specialized in
medieval history and the history of technology. He held academic positions at several colleges and universities in the United States, including
professor of history and director of the Center for Medieval and Renaissance Studies at the University of California—Los Angeles. White was
active in the Presbyterian church throughout his life and was influenced by
his father, who was a Presbyterian professor of Christian ethics. From the
1930s to the 1980s, White was an extremely prolific writer and publisher
of academic articles, magazine essays, and books. The topics he covered
included medieval history, the history of technology, and the connections
between religious belief and the development of technology. During the
1940s he was also known as an outspoken advocate of small colleges,
women's education, and the liberal arts.

In 1967 White published the essay "The Historical Roots of Our
Ecologic Crisis" in *Science*, the peer-reviewed academic journal of the
American Association for the Advancement of Science. In this essay, White

asserted that the Judeo-Christian tradition had culturally predisposed medieval Europe toward a destructive tendency to control nature through technology. Genesis 1:28, which directs humankind to "subdue" the earth and "have dominion" over all living things, was essential to White's argument that the Abrahamic religious traditions, especially Christianity, viewed nature as created to serve the needs of "mankind"

In the "Roots" essay, White further asserts that medieval Christianity's emphasis on human dominance over nature, combined with nineteenth-century Europe's fusion of science and technology, all led to the "ecologic crisis" of the twentieth century. White presents Asian religious traditions as much less exploitative of nature than the Abrahamic traditions, with the exceptions of the Greek Orthodox church and the Catholic Saint Francis of Assisi. White notes that Saint Francis preached the equality of all creatures as well as a revolutionary "pan-psychism" that offers a solution to the destructive Judeo-Christian dominance of nature. White concludes his essay by proposing Saint Francis as the patron saint of ecologists, which eventually occurred in 1979 when Pope John Paul II named Francis of Assisi as the patron saint of those who promote ecology.

Some historians questioned White's evidence and conclusions about religious traditions having destructive attitudes toward nature. Additionally, many scholars and theologians from various religious traditions asserted that White had misinterpreted religious values, practices, and texts. Other critics of White suggested that he had actually made things worse by creating a divide between environmental activists and religious believers. Some critics also suggested that White was legitimizing pantheism or that he was encouraging people to practice animism, Buddhism, and Hinduism. White's "Roots" essay became one of the most-cited articles from *Science* and continues to be noted as a flash point in the study of religion and the environment. His assertions about the role of religion in contemporary environmental problems prompted religious scholars and leaders, theologians, and religious adherents to examine their practices and sacred texts, reflect on their actions, and create guidelines regarding their participation in the contemporary environmental movement.

See also: Religious Environmental Movement

Further Reading

White, Lynn Townsend, Jr. 1971. *Dynamo and Virgin Reconsidered: Essays in the Dynamism of Western Culture*. Cambridge, MA: MIT Press.

World Council of Churches

The World Council of Churches (WCC) is a Christian organization with more than 350 member churches worldwide. WCC programs focus on ecumenism, evangelism, Christian service, justice and peace, integrity of creation, and fostering renewal in Christian unity. Founded in 1948, members initially were Protestant churches from economically developed countries but were soon joined by Orthodox Christian churches and independent churches from around the world. Although the Roman Catholic Church is not a member of the WCC, its cooperation and collaboration with the WCC has increased since the Second Vatican Council. The WCC believes that justice, peace, and environmental protection are interrelated, and it encourages all Christian churches and denominations to collaborate, resist ecological destruction, and create sustainable alternatives to corporate globalization. WCC members participate in programs focused on the natural environment, women, youth, racism, Indigenous peoples, globalization, justice, and peace.

By the 1970s the WCC had begun defining environmental and social justice issues as interrelated "eco-justice" issues, and it has continuously created projects grounded in this concept. The WCC is involved in eco-justice primarily through three main projects: the Ecumenical Water Network; the Climate Justice project; and the Poverty, Wealth and Ecology project. The Ecumenical Water Network provides information to Christian organizations and individuals about the global water crisis and offers community-based solutions; it also advocates for the human right to water. The WCC's Climate Justice project is based on the organization's view that "climate change is as much about inequality in patterns of trade and consumption as it is of increase in greenhouse gas emissions."

As with all environmental issues it addresses, the WCC's work on climate justice is based in the belief that "the Bible teaches the wholeness of creation and calls human beings to take care of the garden of Eden." The Climate Justice project creates ecumenical support for victims of climate change, and the WCC asserts that many corporations are involved in unjust and unsustainable development that contributes to problematic climate change. Similarly, the WCC's Poverty, Wealth and Ecology project focuses on economic inequalities created by economic globalization and encourages Christian advocacy for alternative economic models, such as replacing unsustainable corporate development with locally and regionally sustainable use of resources.

The WCC has continuously provided opportunities for education and advocacy related to Christian-based environmentalism. Seven Weeks for Water is an ongoing project offered during Lent that provides weekly reflections that are distributed globally to WCC member churches and made publicly available. For example, there was a regional focus on Asia during Lent 2019 that included research by a Baptist ecofeminist activist in India on gendered water and women's empowerment, and reflections by WCC members in Malaysia and the Philippines on water for food security and climate adaption. Environmentalism is at the core of almost all WCC efforts, which address "threats to the human community" and encourage "churches to take greater care of creation through protection of the earth and its people."

See also: Christianity; Climate Change; Ecotheology; Environmental Justice

Further Reading

Norwood, Donald W. 2018. *Pilgrimage of Faith: Introducing the World Council of Churches*. Geneva, Switzerland: World Council of Churches Publications.

Annotated Bibliography

The following titles were selected because of their relevance and significance to religion and environmentalism as a field of study. The list is not exhaustive but is representative of the many available works by academics, activists, religious scholars, and other experts. Each entry is composed of a brief description and a statement of its relevance to religion and environmentalism. Author or editor information can be extremely useful for further research and is also included for each title.

Antal, Jim. 2018. *Climate Church, Climate World: How People of Faith Must Work for Change.* **Lanham, MD: Rowman & Littlefield.**
The author, a climate activist, public theologian, and an ordained pastor in the United Church of Christ, argues that climate change is an urgent moral challenge that amplifies all global social injustices. The book presents explanations of why and how people of faith should engage the problem of climate change, from the perspective of an experienced Christian leader and environmental activist. The book provides a brief historical discussion of current environmental problems from a Christian perspective, as well as religion's contributions to creating and worsening these problems. The author then explains that Christianity must embrace environmental activism as a new vocation that is based in biblical scripture and committed to collective salvation. The author advocates for building resilient and sustainable communities, civil disobedience as a Christian act of conscience, and both discipleship and religious revivals focused on care of the natural environment. New approaches to Christian preaching, worship, and witnessing on climate change and sustainability are discussed from the perspective of a religiously motivated environmentalist.

Bartholomew I, Ecumenical Patriarch of Constantinople, and John Chryssavgis. 2012. *On Earth as in Heaven: Ecological Vision and Initiatives of Ecumenical Patriarch Bartholomew.* **Orthodox Christianity and Contemporary Thought. New York: Fordham University Press.**
Bartholomew I of Constantinople has been the ecumenical patriarch of the worldwide Orthodox Christian Church since 1991. In the 1990s, he became known as the "green patriarch" for his commitment to environmental activism in his role as spiritual leader of the world's Orthodox Christians. He has advocated for Christianity's participation in environmentalism and has published extensively on environmentalism. This book is comprised of his selected writings on environmental degradation, global warming, and climate change. The book also includes several of his speeches and interviews, as well as pastoral letters and exhortations, that address environmental issues. It provides insight into the current teachings of the Orthodox Church on environmental issues, and a brief overview of the patriarch's involvement with these issues around the world.

Bstan-'dzin-rgya-mtsho. 2018. *Ecology, Ethics, and Interdependence: The Dalai Lama in Conversation with Leading Thinkers on Climate Change.* **Edited by John Anthony Dunne and Daniel Goleman. Somerville, MA: Wisdom Publications.**
Bstan-'dzin-rgya-mtsho, the current and 14th Dalai Lama, assumed the spiritual title of Dalai Lama in 1939 and at age fifteen officially accepted all political, social, and spiritual duties of the position. This collection of fourteen conversations covers the 14th Dalai Lama's thoughts on environmental ethics, climate change, environmental science and ecology, the status and treatment of all species of animals, the moral and ethical responsibility of religions, Buddhist approaches to environmentalism, environmental activism and related strategies, and environmental sustainability. The conversations are with academics, scientists, physicians, industrial ecologists, Christian theologians, Buddhist leaders, and environmental activists.

Campion, Nicholas. 2016. *The New Age in the Modern West: Counterculture, Utopia and Prophecy from the Late Eighteenth Century to the Present Day.* **New York: Bloomsbury.**
The author is director of the Sophia Centre for the Study of Cosmology in Culture, and program director of the MA in ecology and spirituality at the University of Wales. This book, an intellectual history of the New Age

movement, provides an overview of the philosophers, leaders, gurus, and movements involved in millenarian and utopian beliefs since the Enlightenment. Included are chapters that outline the history of millenarianism and utopianism, two of the most significant terms in New Age thought. Other chapters cover Newton, Voltaire, Swedenborg, transcendentalism, Theosophy, Crowley, Jung, the Beats, esoteric movements, 1960s counterculture, the Punk Movement, science fiction, and other topics and individuals influential in New Age thought. The book also discusses the belief among some New Age groups that an impending global crisis can be averted if enough individuals experience personal enlightenment. An important aspect of this book is the presentation of millennial and utopian thought from diverse philosophical perspectives, many of which have influenced spiritually motivated environmentalism.

Carroll, John, ed. 2016. *The Greening of Faith: God, the Environment, and the Good Life*. Durham: New Hampshire.
Carroll, a professor emeritus of environmental conservation at University of New Hampshire, has published on the topics of agricultural sustainability, ecology, and religion. This anthology has fifteen essays by environmentalists, philosophers, and theologians, written from the perspectives of several world religions and Indigenous spiritual traditions. The essays cover a range of topics, including science and religion, the environment as a spiritual issue, ecumenical and interfaith approaches, domination and environmental suffering, the interrelatedness of all life, sacred ecopsychology, and the religious significance of scientific cosmology. This anthology, originally published in 1996, has an updated preface, foreword, and introduction that discuss the increase in religious environmentalism in the twenty-first century. The essays are of historical interest in the study of religion and the environment, as well as representative of contemporary perspectives toward the natural environment from several religious and spiritual traditions.

Dalton, Anne Marie, and Henry C. Simmons. 2010. *Ecotheology and the Practice of Hope*. SUNY Series on Religion and the Environment. Albany: State University of New York Press.
Anne Dalton is a professor of religious studies at Saint Mary's University, Nova Scotia, and a member of the Interfaith Coalition on Climate Change. Dalton has published several works that cover religion and ecology. Henry Simmons is a professor emeritus of Christian education at Union

Presbyterian Seminary and has written extensively on aging and spirituality. This book provides a concise overview of ecological theology, its various versions, and how it has developed over the past several decades. The authors point out strengths in existing thought in ecotheology and offer suggestions for improvement. They argue that historically ecotheological writings have tended toward pessimism or despair regarding environmental issues but could also offer hope by applying the ideas in ecotheology toward building sustainable societies. Several influential ecological theologians are discussed, including Joseph Sittler, Thomas Berry, Rosemary Radford Ruether, and John Cobb.

Deane-Drummond, Celia E. 2017. *A Primer in Ecotheology: Theology for a Fragile Earth*. Eugene, OR: Cascade (an imprint of Wipf and Stock).
The author, a professor of theology at the University of Notre Dame, is trained as a scientist and theologian who specializes in the dialogue between the sciences and theology. The book provides a thorough overview of the field of ecotheology, with seven chapters that explore different aspects. Topics include anthropocentrism, biocentrism, theocentrism, ecofeminism, creation theology, environmental ethics, political advocacy, and public theology. All of these topics are explored with the assumption that the Bible should be read from an ecological perspective. Contributions by Christian theologians from both Roman Catholicism and Protestantism are discussed, as well as secular debates on environmental issues. The author examines how creation narratives in Genesis are interpreted, including human dominion over other animals. The future of creation is also examined using biblical and other Christian texts and then defined as inseparable from redemption in Christ. The author argues for a theology that views the natural environment as valuable in itself, regardless of human needs and wants. The book also includes a glossary and links to Christian organizations involved in environmental activism.

Delio, Ilia, Keith Douglass Warner, and Pamela Wood. 2008. *Care for Creation: A Franciscan Spirituality of the Earth*. Cincinnati, OH: St. Anthony Messenger Press.
Ilia Delio, a Franciscan Sister of Washington, DC, and theologian, specializes in science and religion, with an emphasis on the theological importance of evolution, physics, and neuroscience. Keith Warner, a member of the Order of Friars Minor (OFM) and director of Education and Action

Research, at Santa Clara University, has research interests in agroecology, ecospirituality, and environmental justice. Pamela Wood is an art therapist, spiritual director, and retreat facilitator focused on Franciscan spirituality and ecological conversion. The authors explore scientific findings on the interdependence of all life and the environmental crisis, and discuss how the life and teachings of Francis of Assisi can provide insight for religiously motivated environmentalism. The book's four sections, on incarnation, community, contemplation, and conversion, present ways to understand humans' place in creation and their role as stewards of the earth. The book includes a biography of Francis of Assisi, an overview of Franciscan ecotheology, scientific research on sustainability, and Franciscan approaches to climate change and other environmental issues.

Drew, Georgina. 2017. *River Dialogues: Hindu Faith and the Political Ecology of Dams on the Sacred Ganga.* **Tucson: University of Arizona Press**.
Drew, a senior lecturer in the Department of Anthropology and Development Studies at the University of Adelaide, researches the cultural and religious politics of resource management. The book is a study of the social movements that have opposed the hydroelectric development of India's sacred Ganga River, and the cultural and religious politics surrounding the reversal of government plans for three major dams on the Ganga River. The includes ethnographical accounts of the women who were core activists in the movement to stop the dam projects. Much of the book is focused on the religious practices, beliefs, and relationships that shaped the politics and environmental stewardship of the activists and other stakeholders. This book provides a clear description and analysis of a recent example of a successful grassroots initiative. Supported with political analysis and ethnographical evidence, this study documents how religiously motivated environmentalism can impact environmental policy as well as reverse corporate and government decisions.

Ellingson, Stephen. 2016. *To Care for Creation: The Emergence of the Religious Environmental Movement.* **Chicago: University of Chicago Press**.
Ellingson, a professor of sociology at Hamilton College, specializes in the sociology of religion, social movements, and sociology of culture. This book provides an overview of the religious environmental movement in the United States, which has become increasingly committed to creating

and practicing a new religiously motivated environmental ethic. Included are discussions about the differences between the religious environmental movement and the secular environmental movement, as well as the strategies of various activists and organizations for overcoming institutional barriers. The author incorporates interviews with more than sixty leaders from several different theological traditions, mostly Christian, to illustrate how activists have mobilized religious believers around environmental issues. Chapters cover the history of the U.S. religious environmental movement, environmentalism as religious mission, the emergence of several different religious environmental traditions, coalition building and political cooperation, and strategic choices in religious social movements. This is one of the most concise, yet detailed, books available on the U.S. religious environmental movement.

Gade, Anna M. 2019. *Muslim Environmentalisms: Religious and Social Foundations.* **New York: Columbia University Press**.
Gade, a scholar of Islam and professor of religious and Asian studies at the University of Wisconsin, researches global environmental issues and conducts related fieldwork in Cambodia, Indonesia, and Malaysia. This book provides an overview of the cultural and religious foundations of Islamic environmentalism, incorporating ethnographic studies and analysis of the empirical, ethical, legal, and social principles that motivate Muslim environmental stewardship. The book includes the author's fieldwork in Southeast Asia and discusses educational programs, international development, case studies in disaster management, Islamic law, religious ritual, and conservation projects, all in the context of Muslim environmentalism. The book includes chapters that cover histories of various Islamic environmentalisms, Qur'anic approaches to animals and natural resources, Islamic humanities, Muslim environmentalism as religious practice, and Islamic environmental justice, law, and ethics.

Gottlieb, Roger S. 2006. *A Greener Faith: Religious Environmentalism and Our Planet's Future.* **New York: Oxford University Press**.
As professor of philosophy at Worcester Polytechnic Institute, Gottlieb's research areas include religious environmentalism, environmental ethics, spirituality in an age of environmental crisis, and the role of religion in a democratic society. The book is an exploration of several themes and topics related to religiously and spiritually motivated environmentalism, and includes some of the author's personal and political views. The history of

the religious environmental movement globally, influential ideas, prominent individuals, and different approaches to environmental activism and sustainability are some of the subjects covered. There are also chapters covering sustainable religion, religious environmentalism in action, environmentalism as spirituality, and the ritual life of religious environmentalism. The author also discusses consumerism, fundamentalism, and globalization, and how religious environmentalists are politically engaged and directly involved in social and economic policies. The book uses examples from around the world and from numerous religions, spiritualities, and cultural traditions.

Hancock, Rosemary. 2017. *Islamic Environmentalism: Activism in the United States and Great Britain*. **London: Taylor & Francis**.
Hancock, a sociologist focused on the intersections of religion, politics, and activism, is a researcher for the Religion and Global Society program at the University of Notre Dame Australia. The book examines Islamic organizations and Muslim activists in the United States and the United Kingdom involved in religiously motivated environmentalism, using social movement theory as an analytical framework. The author incorporates interviews with activists into discussions of environmentalism as religious duty, and documents Muslim environmental activists' use of Islamic scriptures and religious practices as a source of motivation. Topics and themes covered in the book's eight chapters include social movement theory, history and philosophy of the environmental movement, religion and environmentalism, Islamic activism, Muslims and environmentalism, the environment in the Qur'an and Islamic jurisprudence, Muslim intellectuals, Islamic environmental groups and projects, activism and religion, and religious practice as collective action. This is one of the most extensive, detailed, and current books on Islamic environmentalism in the United States and the United Kingdom and is meticulously researched with a bibliography in each chapter.

Harvey, Graham. 2006. *Animism: Respecting the Living World*. **New York: Columbia University Press**.
Professor of religious studies at the Open University, United Kingdom, Harvey's research areas include group identity in ancient Jewish literatures, Pagan identities, Indigenous religions, animism, and ecology. The book covers animism in the contemporary world and incorporates the author's case studies into an exploration of the animistic practices and beliefs of

Aboriginal Australians, Eco-Pagans, Maori, and Native Americans. The first section provides an overview of animism as a concept and term, from its early usage by anthropologists and other scholars to its usage in current academic research. Four case studies on Aboriginal law and land, Eco-Pagan activism, Maori arts, and the Ojibwe and their language constitute the second section. The third section covers animist issues, including personhood of all things in nature, the elements, death as transformation, shamanism, and totemism. The final section details the challenges and issues encountered by contemporary animists, including environmentalism, ecofeminism, feminist and queer persons, and quantum persons. The book is academic, includes a useful bibliography, and has several chapters related to religiously or spiritually motivated environmentalism.

Harvey, Graham. 2011. *Contemporary Paganism: Religions of the Earth from Druids and Witches to Heathens and Ecofeminists.* **New York: New York University Press**.
An experienced researcher in the areas of religious identities, animism, Paganism, and ecology, Harvey explores and documents contemporary Paganism in detail. This book is an introduction to contemporary Paganism and its most prominent forms in thirteen distinct chapters. The author uses historical, scientific, and anthropological sources, as well as literature and sources at the core of various Pagan belief systems. Beginning with the Pagan calendar and its seasons, there are clear explanations of the Wheel of the Year, solstice, equinox, lunar cycles, star lore, and related Pagan beliefs and celebrations. There are separate chapters for contemporary Druids, Wiccans, Heathens, Goddess spiritualty, Esotericism, and Shamanism, with each including historical background, beliefs and practices, organizational size and structure, and bibliographies. Chapters also cover Paganism and ecology, including various examples of Pagan environmental activism and Pagan approaches in environmental sustainability. The remainder of the book includes discussions of sacred natural sites, sacred geometry, Gaia theory, ecology and theology, historical sources, rites of passage, Paganism and interfaith dialogue, and researching Paganism. Throughout the book, examples are included that illustrate the importance of both individual needs and social relationships in Paganism.

Jain, Pankaj. 2016. *Dharma and Ecology of Hindu Communities: Sustenance and Sustainability.* **London: Routledge**.

A professor of philosophy and religion at the University of North Texas, Jain's research and publication areas include environmental issues and movements in India, Sanskrit language and literature, religion and ecology, and sustainability of religious communities in the Americas. This book presents research on three communities in India—the Svadhyaya movement, the Bishnoi community, and the Bhil tribal community—and a discussion of the South Asian ethos of dharma as a method for coping with environmental issues. The author discusses the Svadhyaya movement, which promotes tree planting and mass literacy campaigns inspired by the Bhagavad Gita, as an example of environmental consciousness motivated by religious devotion. The Bishnoi community, known for protecting animals and forests, is discussed as the inspiration for the Chipko movement, which protected forests from corporate destruction in the twentieth century. The third community, the Bhil tribe, is known for protecting sacred groves in cooperation with India's government. In all three cases, the author explains and provides examples of how religious communities are involved in environmentalist activism.

Johnston, Lucas F. 2014. *Religion and Sustainability: Social Movements and the Politics of the Environment*. Hoboken, NJ: Taylor & Francis.
The author, a professor of religion and environmental studies at Wake Forest University, has research and publications focused on biocultural evolution and religion, environmental social movements, and political discourse about nature. The book examines the ways that religious and spiritual discourse influence sustainability politics, and the different ways that religious and secular groups define and apply the concept of sustainability. The first two sections of the book, constituting six chapters, are dedicated to defining religion and sustainability, presenting a history of the sustainability movement, and describing sustainability as expressed in religions, civil society, international politics, and the natural and social sciences. The remaining third section includes three case studies: how evangelical Christian elites developed a theology and practice of environmental sustainability; how interfaith organizations connect religious and nonreligious groups on sustainability issues; and analysis of interview data to demonstrate the presence of religion in secular environmentalists and organizations. The book includes coverage of social movement theory, theories of sustainability, and the influence of religion in politics.

Kearns, Laurel, and Catherine Keller, eds. 2007. *Ecospirit: Religions and Philosophies for the Earth.* **New York: Fordham University Press**.
Kearns, a professor of sociology and religion and environmental studies at Drew University, has researched and published on religion and environmentalism, nature spirituality, and religious responses to global warming. Keller, a professor of constructive theology at Drew University, specializes in ecological and gender politics, cosmology, and philosophy and religious pluralism. This book is a collection of essays written by the editors and several additional authors from several different disciplines, fields of study, and perspectives. The introduction helps readers understand the purpose of the book, which aims at exploring new ways of thinking about identity, religion, transnational collaboration, communities that include all living things, all in the context of environmentalism and ecology. The book has six sections with several chapters in each that cover themes in language, science, theology, spirit, place, and enactment. While a few of the essays are written for academic audiences, most of the essays are accessible to a wide range of readers and address specific environmental issues, such as biodiversity, deforestation, global warming, interspecies relations, and the Alaska National Wildlife Refuge.

Kent, Eliza F. 2013. *Sacred Groves and Local Gods: Religion and Environmentalism in South India.* **Oxford: Oxford University Press**.
Kent, a professor of religion at Skidmore College, has researched and published on South Asian religions, religion and ecology, religious environmentalism, and related topics. The book is based on the author's fieldwork and provides historical background and analysis of the social, political, and religious context of the religious environmentalism of five communities in the Tamil Nadu region. The introduction is a brief overview of sacred groves and the local deities associated with them, as well as a general discussion of religious environmentalism in South India and its contribution to forest conservation. Five chapters present case studies on sacred groves and religious environmentalism in several locations: near Madurai; Malaiyali; the Pondicherry region; the Auroville Plateau; and the sacred grove restoration projects near Chennai. The locations range from subsistence agrarian to more modernized regions, with farmers, villagers, emerging generations influenced by urban development, and a complex diversity of religiously motivated communities who provide care for the sacred groves. The impact of globalization and economic development on the sacred groves is also explained.

Khalid, Fazlun M. 2019. *Signs on the Earth: Islam, Modernity and the Climate Crisis*. Markfield, UK: Kube Publishing.
Khalid, founder and director of the Islamic Foundation for Ecology and Environmental Science (IFEES), has written and published several works on Islam and environmentalism and has worked for several environmental organizations, including the Alliance of Religions and Conservation (ARC) and the World Wildlife Fund (WWF). The book covers globalization, economic development, advances in science, the environmental responsibilities of Muslims, and the disputed values of modernity and consumerism. The six chapters include discussions of the disruption of traditional societies, the contemporary degradation of ecosystems, the illusory and real aspects of progress, and environmentalism as mandated in Islamic sacred texts and tradition. In several persuasive appeals, the author requests that Muslims, people of other faiths, and those who are not religious or spiritual, should work together to preserve and protect the natural environment for future generations. The book includes a bibliography, an appendix with the Islamic Declaration on Global Climate Change, a glossary of Arabic terms, and a list of quotations from the Qur'an.

LeVasseur, Todd, Pramod Parajuli, and Norman Wirzba, eds. 2016. *Religion and Sustainable Agriculture: World Spiritual Traditions and Food Ethics*. Lexington: University Press of Kentucky.
LeVasseur is a professor of religious studies and environmental sustainability studies at the College of Charleston. Parajuli, faculty in sustainability education at Prescott College, has researched and published on political ecology, religion and ecology, and sustainability education. Wirzba, a professor of theology at Duke Divinity School, specializes in theology, philosophy, ecology, and agrarian and environmental studies. The book covers the relationships among religious beliefs and sustainable agriculture practices in seventeen essays by activists, lay farmers, scholars, and theologians, including a foreword by environmental activist and scientist Vandana Shiva. The essays include Indigenous, Buddhist, Christian, Hindu, Jewish, and Muslim perspectives on how religious beliefs influence the practices and values in sustainable agriculture. Some of the issues examined include environmental justice, global trade agreements, the effects of postcolonialism, and Indigenous land and seed rights. The essays include case studies from numerous locations, including Europe, Egypt, El Salvador, Guatemala, Hawaii, India, Israel, Malawi, Peru, and Thailand.

Lovelock, James. 1995. *Gaia: A New Look at Life on Earth***. Oxford: Oxford University Press**.

Lovelock has held several positions in medical research and academic departments since the 1950s, invented the electron capture detector that enabled the detection of nano-pollutants, and is the originator of Gaia theory. The author has written several environmental science books based on the Gaia theory, with this book being a reissue and revision of the original 1979 edition. The book, consisting of nine chapters written with the general public in mind, includes discussions of scientific knowledge related to contemporary environmental challenges, cybernetics, the atmosphere, the sea, and pollution. The book presents the author's Gaia hypothesis, which includes three core assertions about the earth: that it is composed of various living entities and nonliving parts that are all interdependent in a self-regulating system; that it is in a state of equilibrium, and if anything changes then it affects the entire system and its parts, resulting in imbalance; and that its largest living creature is Gaia, which has organs, such as atmosphere, oceans, wetlands, or rainforests, that are all interdependent and essential to sustaining life.

McDuff, Mallory. 2014. *Sacred Acts: How Churches Are Working to Protect Earth's Climate***. Gabriola Island, Canada: New Society**.

McDuff is a professor of outdoor leadership and environmental studies, and director of environmental education at Warren Wilson College, with research interests in faith communities, climate action, and integrating local communities into environmental education. This book focuses on climate change and explains how churches can "care for the Creation" by addressing environmental issues. The book has an introduction by McDuff followed by twelve essays arranged into four sections on stewardship, spirituality, advocacy, and justice. The essays are written for a broad audience from a Christian perspective by activists in the environmental movement, clergy, and academics. Community farming, critical comments by evangelical climate scientists, Christian responses to the dangers of coal and mountaintop removal mining, social justice issues in climate-caused immigration, and the importance of prayer and action for victims of natural disasters are some of the topics covered in these essays. The book presents a range of experiences from the lives of Christian environmentalists in the United States, with an emphasis on community-based responses and solutions to climate change.

Miller, James. 2017. *China's Green Religion: Daoism and the Quest for a Sustainable Future.* **New York: Columbia University Press**.
Miller, professor of humanities at Duke Kunshan University, conducts research and publishes on religion and ecology in China and on the Daoist religion. The author examines China's Indigenous Daoist tradition and environmental sustainability, using recent scholarship, science, new definitions of religion, and postcolonial theoretical approaches. One of the purposes of the book is to rethink both Daoism and sustainability, using historical Daoist ideas to inform a new way of thinking about environmental problems. This emphasis is on Daoism, but informed discussions of other religious and spiritual traditions are included. The book's eight chapters examine Daoism in the context of modernity, ecology, nature, the body, location, and sustainability. The author argues that Daoism can provide insights for environmentalists, such as recognizing the interconnections between nature and culture, and the idea that the natural environment supports human flourishing. The book is written for academics and policy makers but is also an advanced authoritative source for other students of Daoism and environmentalism.

Nasr, Seyyed Hossein. 1990. *Man and Nature: The Spiritual Crisis in Modern Man.* **London: Unwin**.
Nasr, a professor of Islamic studies, religion, and philosophy at George Washington University, is a prominent, globally recognized scholar of numerous subjects, including ecology, the natural environment, the history and philosophy of science, metaphysics, ethics, art and aesthetics, comparative religion, and mysticism. This book is based on lectures the author delivered in 1966 at the University of Chicago that explore different religious traditions' understanding of the relationship between humans and nature, with particular attention given to Sufism. The author asserts that, to solve environmental problems, humans must have a metaphysical and spiritual understanding of nature. The author provides historical context for environmental problems and explains that humans should try to live in harmony with nature rather than dominate it. Using the Sufi tradition as an example, the author suggests that religious mysticism can provide insight into current social and environmental problems. The author includes a critique of materialism and discusses how modern science has forgotten its sacred origins. The book contains transcriptions of scholarly lectures that provide insight into how Sufism and Islamic philosophy approach environmentalism.

Nelson, Melissa K., and Dan Shilling, eds. 2018. *Traditional Ecological Knowledge: Learning from Indigenous Practices for Environmental Sustainability*. New York: Cambridge University Press.
Nelson, a professor of American Indian Studies at San Francisco State University and an Anishinaabe/Métis/Norwegian-enrolled member of the Turtle Mountain Band of Chippewa Indians, specializes in the areas of Indigenous rights, Native science and biocultural diversity, ecological ethics, and sustainability. Shilling is a faculty member at Arizona State University's Sustainability and the Humanities Institute who writes on environmental issues and helps communities preserve their culture and natural environment. This book is a collection of essays on traditional ecological knowledge (TEK) written by scholars from various disciplines. An introductory chapter provides key concepts and definitions in the study of TEK, followed by fourteen essays written mostly by Indigenous scientists. The essays are arranged in four sections that cover key concepts and questions, philosophical foundations, land care practices and plant and animal relationships, and the global and legal implications of Indigenous sustainability. The essays cover environmental sustainability and belief systems as practiced in several different geographic and tribal contexts across North America, Australia, and other regions.

Rankin, Aidan. 2018. *Jainism and Environmental Philosophy: Karma and the Web of Life*. London: Taylor & Francis.
Rankin is a researcher, independent scholar, and writer in the areas of Indian philosophy and spirituality, Jainism, shamanic and Indigenous traditions, Shinto, and ethical science. In general, the book explains how being a Jain can contribute to environmentalism and how the Jain beliefs in nonviolence and the reduction of harm support environmental sustainability. The book's six chapters provide an introduction to Jain thought and practice, the relevance of Jainism, the ecology of karma, diversity and unity, Jain businesses and environmental ethics, and a conclusion that sums up key points. The author presents Jain thought as a system of values that prioritizes environmental protection and the interconnectedness of all life. The author suggests that Jain environmentalism, which evolved in India, has beliefs and practices that can provide insight into sustainability and other environmental issues. The book includes discussions of interest to readers interested in religion and environmentalism as well as more focused scholarship on Jainism, environmental ethics and policy, and sustainable economics.

Rots, Aike P. 2017. *Shinto, Nature and Ideology in Contemporary Japan: Making Sacred Forests*. **London: Bloomsbury Publishing**.
Rots is a professor of Japan studies at the University of Oslo, with research and publications on popular and Indigenous religion, environmental activism, multispecies relations, the politics of cultural and natural heritage, Shinto and shrine rituals, and religious environmentalism in Japan, Vietnam, and the Ryukyu Islands. This book, a systematic study of Shinto and environmentalism, explains how Shinto has contributed to global environmentalism and engaged international organizations that protect sacred sites. The author's ethnographic research in Japan between 2011 and 2013 is incorporated throughout the book, and provides examples of Shinto's influence among scientists, priests, new religious movements, and religiously motivated environmentalism in Japan. Topics and themes covered in the book's twelve chapters include Shinto definitions and concepts; love of nature; the Shinto environmentalist paradigm; *chinju no mori* (sacred shrine forests); landscapes; future forests; rebuilding sacred forests destroyed by natural disaster; and Shinto's global involvement in environmentalism. The book is written with several audiences in mind and provides clear examples of religiously motivated environmentalism in contemporary Shinto beliefs and practices.

Ruether, Rosemary Radford. 2005. *Integrating Ecofeminism, Globalization, and World Religions*. **Lanham, MD: Rowman & Littlefield**.
Ruether is a professor emerita of feminist theology at the Pacific School of Religion and the Graduate Theological Union in Berkeley, and is an activist, scholar, teacher, and ecofeminist theologian in the Roman Catholic Church. This book takes an ecofeminist approach to religion and spirituality and focuses on corporate globalization, interfaith ecological theory, and ecofeminism. The first chapter defines corporate globalization and provides an ecofeminist critique of its effects. The second chapter explores how major world religions have been involved in environmental degradation in the past yet have recently become involved in environmentalism. Feminist theory, theology, and the emergence of ecofeminism are covered in the third chapter, which also discusses the historical domination of women and nature. The fourth and final chapter examines alternatives to corporate globalization, providing contemporary examples of resistance such as the Zapatista movement and protests against the World Trade Organization. Throughout the book, the author provides definitions and contexts for theories and theologies and uses contemporary examples to illustrate points.

Shafiq, Muhammad, and Thomas Herrold Donlin-Smith, eds. 2018. *Nature and the Environment in Contemporary Religious Contexts.* **Newcastle upon Tyne, UK: Cambridge Scholars Publishing**.
Shafiq is a professor of religious studies at Nazareth College, with research and publications in the area of comparative religion, Islamic studies, and interfaith studies. Donlin-Smith is a professor of religious studies at Nazareth College, with special interests in comparative religious ethics, bioethics, and religion and science. The book is a collection of seventeen essays from the perspectives of the social sciences and religion on human relationships with the natural environment. The essays cover several topics, such as the contemporary environmental crisis, industrialization, waste management, interspecies relationships, dharma, environmental stewardship, and human interdependence with the natural world. The essays, which represent the perspectives of several world religions and a few Indigenous spiritualities, are arranged in three sections that cover human contexts within nature, imperatives from sacred texts and traditions, and practicing the imperatives. The essays are scholarly, researched, and were originally peer-reviewed articles presented at a conference on nature, the environment, and religions at the Hickey Center for Interfaith Studies and Dialogue at Nazareth College.

Taylor, Bron Raymond, ed. 2005. *The Encyclopedia of Religion and Nature.* **London and New York: Thoemmes Continuum**.
Taylor, a professor of religion at the University of Florida and founder of the *Journal for the Study of Religion, Nature and Culture*, researches and publishes on religion and nature, environmental and social ethics, and environmental movements and politics. Consisting of two volumes, this encyclopedia is the current authoritative source on religion and nature, covering ecology, theology, significant individuals and events, religious traditions and organizations, philosophy, and a range of other related themes and topics. There are 1,000 entries by 520 contributors from around the world, including both scholarly academic entries and entries by influential religious practitioners. This encyclopedia includes an extensive and informative introduction that provides definitions of religion, nature, and nature religion, and a history of the evolution of the interest in religion and nature. The introduction also discusses religion and nature in the environmental age, world religions and environmentalism, and the future of nature and religion.

Taylor, Bron Raymond. 2010. *Dark Green Religion: Nature Spirituality and the Planetary Future.* **Berkeley: University of California Press**.
Taylor, a professor of religion at the University of Florida and founder of the *Journal for the Study of Religion, Nature and Culture*, researches and publishes on religion and nature, environmental and social ethics, and environmental movements and politics. This book defines and examines contemporary "green religions" that view nature and the natural world as sacred, including both traditional religions and new spiritual practices that have replaced them. The book's nine chapters cover terms and concepts, the history of nature religion, animism, Gaia theory, traditional ecological knowledge (TEK), radical environmentalism as a type of dark green religion, surfing and nature spirituality, globalization, global earth religion, and the future impact of dark green religion. Included is the author's broad definition of religion, which has created opportunities for an expanded understanding of religious environmentalism, ranging from predominant world religions to obscure "religious-resembling" communities. Written for an academic audience, many sections of the book are accessible to a broad audience interested in religion, religious-resembling communities, and environmentalism.

Teilhard de Chardin, Pierre. 2002. *The Phenomenon of Man.* **New York: Perennial Library**.
Teilhard de Chardin was a Jesuit priest, mystic, paleontologist, and geologist who conducted scientific research, taught at universities, and wrote on evolution and spirituality. The author asserts that planetary history, human evolution, and love of all living things are essential elements of the Omega Point, which is the final point of divine unification of all things in the universe. The author theorizes that all life and forms of life throughout time are part of a divinely planned evolution that culminates in all things merging with the Cosmic Christ at the Omega Point. This book introduces some of the author's most influential philosophical and theological ideas, including that the planet has evolved distinct layers over time: first, the geosphere; then the biosphere; then the noösphere; and ultimately a theosphere, in the future. The author asserts that the planet's currently evolving layer is the noösphere, or layer of mind and spirit, which is the collective emergence of all human thought. This is a seminal work that influenced many important theologians, religious environmentalists, scientists, and pioneers of cyberspace and the internet.

Tirosh-Samuelson, Hava, ed. 2002. *Judaism and Ecology: Created World and Revealed Word.* **Cambridge, MA: Harvard University Press**. Director of Jewish Studies and professor of modern Judaism at Arizona State University, Tirosh-Samuelson's interests include Jewish intellectual history, the interaction between Judaism, Christianity, and Islam in the Middle Ages, bioethics, and Judaism and ecology. This is a collection of twenty-one essays by religious scholars, theologians, and academics on topics related to Jewish theology of nature. The book is divided into six sections: Constructive Jewish Theology of Nature; The Human Condition: Origins, Pollution, and Death; The Doctrine of Creation; Nature and Revealed Morality; Nature in Jewish Mysticism; and From Speculation to Action. The essays provide insight into how rabbinical and sacred texts inform contemporary Jewish approaches to the natural environment and environmentalism. The last two essays, "Can Judaism Make Environmental Policy? Sacred and Secular Language in Jewish Ecological Discourse" and "Jewish Environmentalism: Past Accomplishments and Future Challenges," provide some of the most concise analysis and histories of Jewish environmentalism currently available. Most of the essays are accessible to a wide range of readers.

Walters, Kerry S., and Lisa Portmess, eds. 2001. *Religious Vegetarianism: From Hesiod to the Dalai Lama.* **Albany: State University of New York Press**.
Walters, a professor emeritus of philosophy at Gettysburg College and a priest in the American National Catholic Church, has publications on numerous topics, including Christian mysticism, atheism, the ethics of diet, Christian pacifism, and American history. Portmess, a professor of philosophy at Gettysburg College, specializes in philosophy of language, philosophy of technology, philosophy of mind, world philosophy, and peace and justice studies. This book is a collection of writings on religious vegetarianism by classic, historical, and contemporary thinkers from Buddhist, Christian, Indian, Islamic, Jewish, and Pythagorean traditions. Explanations, descriptions, and an historical overview of the writings are provided in an introduction by the editors. The book includes discussions within traditions over use of animals for food purposes, religious law and tradition positions on vegetarianism, the status of all animals as members of creation, and the relationship between humans and the natural environment. This collection is useful as a sourcebook for beginning scholars, advanced scholars new to the topic, and the general public.

Weeramantry, C. G. 2009. *Tread Lightly on the Earth: Religion, the Environment, and the Human Future: A Report for the World Future Council.* **Pannipitiya, Sri Lanka: Stamford Lake**.
Weeramantry, a professor emeritus of law at Monash University and a former justice of the Supreme Court of Sri Lanka, published on numerous topics, among them, Islamic jurisprudence, international law and human rights, comparative law, sustainable justice, environmental damage, and ethics in science. The book consists of eleven chapters that describe and examine contemporary environmental issues, the Assisi Declarations of 1986, and core teachings related to the natural environment in Buddhism, Christianity, Hinduism, Islam, and Judaism. The author also identifies and discusses worldviews focused on short-term economic profits, which have contributed to environmental problems. Other issues discussed include economic privilege, national sovereignty, rights versus duties, and human use of global natural resources. Throughout the book, the author asserts that religious traditions are a source of knowledge that can be used to create an environmentally, socially, and economically sustainable world.

White, Lynn Townsend, Jr. 1971. *Dynamo and Virgin Reconsidered: Essays in the Dynamism of Western Culture.* **Cambridge, MA: MIT Press**.
The author was a historian who specialized in medieval history and the history of technology. He held academic positions at several colleges and universities in the United States, including professor of history and director of the Center for Medieval and Renaissance Studies at the University of California—Los Angeles. This collection of eleven historical essays explores the relationship between technology, society, religion, and science in medieval Europe. Included is White's 1967 essay, "The Historical Roots of Our Ecologic Crisis," in which the author asserts that the Judeo-Christian tradition had culturally predisposed medieval Europe toward a destructive tendency to control nature through technology. Because of the many responses it generated from religious scholars in Judaism and Christianity, the "Roots" essay continues to be noted as a flash point in the study of religion and the environment.

Witt, Joseph. 2016. *Religion and Resistance in Appalachia: Faith and the Fight Against Mountaintop Removal Coal Mining.* **Lexington: University Press of Kentucky**.
A professor of religion at Mississippi State University, Witt's research and publication topics include religious and environmental attitudes and

behaviors, environmental activism, environmental ethics, and food security in the U.S. South. This book explores the relationship between religion and environmental activism through the example of resistance in Appalachia to mountaintop removal coal mining. The author's historical research and fieldwork provides readers with the context needed to understand the numerous interviews with activists, educators, pastors, and community leaders involved in religiously motivated environmentalism. The interview excerpts included throughout the book are from adherents in Indigenous and nontraditional spiritual traditions, Catholic and Protestant social justice activists, and evangelical Christians. The book's introduction, five chapters, and conclusion cover religion and place, religions and environmental justice, religious environmental stewardship, biocentrism and nature-based spiritualities, cultural interaction, and the future of religiously motivated environmentalism. Included also are religious debates, such as the tension between those who assert that the earth should be protected and those who assert that God gave humans coal for comfort and prosperity.

World Wildlife Fund. 1986. *The Assisi Declarations: Messages on Man & Nature from Buddhism, Christianity, Hinduism, Islam and Judaism.* **Gland, Switzerland: World Wildlife Fund**.
The World Wildlife Fund, known outside of Canada and the United States as the World Wide Fund for Nature, is the world's largest international, nongovernmental conservation organization. Founded in 1961, WWF has worked with several religious organizations on environmental issues. In collaboration with the Alliance of Religions and Conservation (ARC) and the WWF, this publication was written by leaders from five major world religions: Lungrig Rinpoche, abbot of Gyuto Tantric University (Buddhist); Lanfranco Serrini, minister general of the Franciscan Order of Friars Minor (Christianity); Karan Singh, president of the Hindu Virat Samaj (Hindu); Abdullah Omar Naseef, secretary general of the Muslim World League (Islam); and Arthur Hertzberg, vice president of the World Jewish Congress (Judaism). These leaders contributed to this document as part of their participation in the 1986 WWF meeting in Assisi, Italy, which addressed the role of religion in protecting and saving the natural world from environmental crisis. The leaders from the five contributing religions outline their tradition's distinct approach to ecology, environmentalism, and care for the natural world.

Yoreh, Tanhum. 2019. *Waste Not: A Jewish Environmental Ethic.* **Albany: State University of New York Press.**
Yoreh, a professor in the School of the Environment at the University of Toronto, researches and publishes on the intellectual history of religiously motivated environmentalism, religious legal approaches to environmental policy, and approaches to wastefulness in the Abrahamic faiths. This book uses sacred texts and commentaries in Judaism to support a contemporary Jewish approach to environmental ethics. The book's emphasis is on the Jewish law of *bal tashḥit*, which is the prohibition against destruction and wastefulness. The author provides a history of the concept through classical rabbinical literature, Jewish law, and the writings of contemporary environmentalists. Topics covered include Jewish perspectives on sustainable food practices, environmental protection, and environmental law, and the author explores how these perspectives can inform Jewish environmentalism. The book includes definitions and excerpts from rabbinical literature and sacred texts and is written with the general public, special interest groups, and scholarly audiences in mind.

Index

Page numbers in **bold** indicate the location of main entries.

About the Author

LORA STONE is associate professor of sociology at the University of New Mexico-Gallup. She has contributed to works including *Reforming America: A Thematic Encyclopedia and Document Collection of the Progressive Era*; and *Imperialism and Expansionism in American History: A Social, Political, and Cultural Encyclopedia and Document Collection*; and *Encyclopedia of American Religion and Politics*. She has conducted national research on congregational development and political participation as well as regional research on culture and environmentalism in youth conservation corps.